# Astrals, Auras & Apparitions: A Compendium of the Paranormal

BY

JUDITH ENNAMORATO

PARAPSYCHOLOGIST AND PSYCHIC RESEARCHER

Note for Librarians: A cataloguing record for this book is available from Library and Archives Canada at www.collectionscanada.ca/amicus/index-e.html
ISBN 1-4120-8370-2

*Trafford's print shop runs on "green energy" from solar, wind and other environmentally-friendly power sources.*

*Offices in Canada, USA, Ireland and UK*

**Book sales for North America and international:**
Trafford Publishing, 6E–2333 Government St.,
Victoria, BC V8T 4P4 CANADA
phone 250 383 6864 (toll-free 1 888 232 4444)
fax 250 383 6804; email to orders@trafford.com
**Book sales in Europe:**
Trafford Publishing (UK) Limited, 9 Park End Street, 2nd Floor
Oxford, UK OX1 1HH UNITED KINGDOM
phone 44 (0)1865 722 113 (local rate 0845 230 9601)
facsimile 44 (0)1865 722 868; info.uk@trafford.com
**Order online at:**
trafford.com/06-0125

10 9 8 7 6 5 4 3 2

# Dedication

This book is dedicated to the memory of my dear grandmother, Irene Whitehead, who taught me not to fear the unknown, as it is simply proof of the continuation of our existence.

# Acknowledgements

For many years now, I have been contemplating the writing of this book, mainly because the contents envelop such an enormous segment of my life thus far. I wish to thank those individuals who so graciously recounted their psychic experiences with me, however uncomfortable it was for them at the time.

To avoid footnotes when citing other material, references to most sources have been kept within the narrative and can be used for further reading.

On a more personal note, thanks to my beautiful family for their never-ending encouragement in terms of my literary endeavors.

Judith Ennamorato
Schomberg, Ontario
April 4, 2006

# Contents

# PREFACE

*We prefer to deny that which we cannot explain...*

For the second time that day the local undertaker vacated the grandiose, one hundred and fifty-year-old Edwardian mansion situated on the shore of beautiful Lake Ontario. This time, however, he wasn't alone in the hearse. Wrapped tightly in a makeshift shroud, the body of a newborn girl lay behind him as he made his way along the sinuous driveway lined on either side by towering maples and firs. Covered in shattered clamshells by the infant's grandfather in order to beautify the property, the driveway had been magically transformed into a glistening trail of mother-of-pearl as a result of the brilliant October sun.

Surrounded by a riot of fall colors, he reflected on the day's events beginning with the initial call to the funeral home early that morning. The grandmother was requesting his immediate assistance as her daughter-in-law had just given birth to an infant girl whose life, according to the doctor who had delivered her, was to end momentarily. The terrified cries of the new mother could be heard in the background, "Get a priest, get a priest, she's going to go to hell!"

He would later learn that during the delivery, the doctor had declared it to be a "footling birth" in that both feet appeared as opposed to a "normal birth" where the head presents itself first. However, in this case, only one foot had emerged and the doctor, in an attempt to release the other foot, yanked on the exposed limb, unaware its counterpart was tangled in the umbilical cord. As a result, the infant's reproductive organs had been ripped to shreds. The loss of blood was enormous. The grandmother, trained as a practical nurse, knew the baby would never survive the lengthy trip to a hospital. Hastily retrieving her sewing box, she proceeded to stitch together the tiny pieces of torn flesh without (of course) the aid of any anesthetic. Halfway through the procedure the infant expired and was pronounced clinically dead by the doctor. The tiny, lifeless body had been bound tightly in a sheet and put aside to await the arrival of the local undertaker.

Arriving at the home a few hours later, he'd been escorted by the maid into the lavish dining room where the superb mahogany table had been hastily transformed into a makeshift delivery table. There he was informed that the infant, dead for over an hour, had suddenly begun crying. The local priest was hastily summoned to baptize the infant lest she expire again and (according to her mother's religious beliefs) go to hell.

Wishing the family all the best, the undertaker returned to the funeral home a few blocks away. Later that day he was summoned once again to the mansion on the lake where he was informed that the priest had arrived; however, halfway through the baptismal rites the infant had succumbed for the second time. The grandmother would later recount how the priest had paused during the holy sacrament before raising his arm toward the heavens and declaring, "I'm sorry, she's passed over."

Arriving back at the mansion a few hours later, he retrieved the dead infant from the arms of her grandmother. He felt the tears welling up in his eyes. As a close friend of the family, he was only too aware that the infant's mother had previously lost other children at birth—a daughter and twin boys.

Pulling into the driveway of the funeral home, he made his way to the back of the hearse to fetch the dead infant when he heard the sound of a faint whimper. With shaking hands he cautiously removed the covering from the baby. She was staring up at him. She was breathing once again. He couldn't believe it. In all his years as a mortician he'd never experienced anything like this. The infant had succumbed twice, both for substantial amounts of time; yet, here she was, alive and breathing. Hastily returning to the family mansion he watched as the grandmother and mother, sobbing with happiness, cuddled the infant.

The grandmother completed the necessary operation to the best of her ability, binding the infant's legs tightly together lest the stitches rip. A few days later a nurse from the Victorian Order arrived at the mansion to assist in the infant's care. Removing the binding from the tiny legs, she lifted the infant from the bed to further scrutinize the horrendous damage that had occurred during birth. Shaking her head back and forth, she looked at the grandmother before stating in a matter-of-fact tone, "This infant will never survive."

With that, she carelessly tossed the baby onto the bed, and in doing so, the infant's legs splayed apart, ripping out every stitch so lovingly placed by the distraught grandmother. Furious, the older woman grabbed the nurse by her collar and proceeded to toss her down the winding staircase before once again retrieving her sewing box and operating as best she could on the tiny baby girl.

From the time she was able to talk, the child would relate to her family, the "people" she had seen roaming through the great house at all hours of the day and night, describing in detail their manner of period dress. She would delight in telling her grandmother how the women wore long skirts and lovely wide-brimmed hats. It would appear that her "death experiences" had modified her consciousness in such a way as to allow her to see spirits. Marking these visions down to common childhood dreams, most of her family listened to her stories with tongue-in-cheek; all that is, except her grandmother who'd had her own share of psychic experiences during her lifetime. She understood the child, never scoffing at her encounters with the apparitions, comforting her instead when "the bad lady" (as the child called her) appeared to her at night just before sleep.

Alerted to a hissing sound at the door of her bedroom, the child would look up to see a stout, white-haired, middle-aged woman with outstretched arms and clenched fists walking toward her bed, a ghastly hissing sound emanating from behind her clenched teeth. It was at these times she'd leap from her bed to snuggle against her grandmother who would soothe her until she slept. On one of these occasions, the child was just about to fall asleep in her grandmother's arms when she was alerted to the presence of two males leaning over the bed on her grandfather's side. Not wanting to wake him, she shook her grandmother awake.

"Mommie," she whispered, "Who are they?" Glancing toward the side of the bed where her husband slept, her grandmother promptly reached over the little girl to shake her husband awake.

"Frank...Frank, wake up...look...what is that?"

Awakening with a start, her grandfather opened his eyes, and looked to the side of the bed where the spirits stood. Startled, he swung his arm through them while uttering, "Jesus Christ!"

Within a matter of seconds, the apparitions slowly dissipated and the little girl, with a smile on her lips, thought to herself, *No one can make fun of me anymore because my Mommie and Pop-pop saw the ghosts too!*

The incident was never mentioned after that, and as the girl matured, she recognized the fact that her grandfather's prominent standing in the community, both as a businessman and church leader, would prevent him from divulging the experience to the general public for fear of discrediting his mental stability.

At the age of three the little girl moved to Buffalo, New York with her parents and older brother. One night she awoke to find her room rather dimly lit in an exquisite emerald shade. Leaning over her bed were the figures of three bearded men, their mouths covered with, what she learned later in life, were surgeon's masks. One of the men held a lantern over her from which shone an odd sparkling light. She could hear them mumbling, but couldn't make out the words. Their eyes looked sad as they stared down at her, shaking their heads as if there was something terribly wrong with her, or worse yet, as if to imply she'd just passed away.

The child, not knowing they were spirits, wondered who these bearded men with the kind eyes were. She knew better than to discuss the incident with her mother who, for reasons the child didn't understand, became angered at the mention of her visions. She'd later realize that her mother had a fear of "ghosts" so the child kept the information to herself. During the next year or so the exact scene was played out in her emerald green room many times. She was never afraid of the kind men, who obviously cared for her safety. Many years later, she would watch a television documentary describing how the doctors, during the era of the Civil War, had often resorted to placing fireflies inside their lanterns for light. *But what had she to do with the Civil War?*

When she was five her family moved back to Ontario and she was once again living in the mansion with her adored grandmother. On a couple of occasions, a relative would appear to her at night, standing at the foot of the bed, smiling lovingly at her until she slept. Inevitably, these relatives appeared to her at the time of their death hundreds of miles away.

Baby dolls were her most precious possessions and she played with them constantly, waiting for the day when she would grow up, marry and have real babies of her own; but apparently that was not meant to be. As soon as she was able to comprehend such things, her grandmother tenderly informed her that she could never give birth to a baby as her internal organs had been damaged during her birth. This didn't bother the child too much as her grandmother assured her that she could adopt a baby—or babies—and raise them as her own. As well, the doctor who had delivered her reminded her of this whenever she went to his office for a check-up, which was quite often during her formative years. An active child, she'd had a couple of nasty falls while attempting to climb trees. Her mother, grandmother or doctor always examined her immediately following these accidents.

At the age of eighteen she became engaged to her high-school sweetheart. She informed him that she could never get pregnant let alone give birth. He understood and agreed wholeheartedly that they would adopt since they both loved children and wished to have many of them. Before the wedding, her grandmother advised her to see a gynecologist. Once there, she gave him her history, at which point he inquired if she was aware that she would never have children. She assured him she had known that for many years.

They married in October and ten months later, almost to the day, she gave birth to a beautiful, healthy baby boy.

Dreams had always played a large role in the child's life and though she had more than her fair share of nightmares, her precognitive dreams always foretold of pleasant events that usually materialized within three months of the prophecy.

About six months following the birth of her son, she dreamed of giving birth to twin girls. In the dream, the doctor was telling her that one of the infants had to stay in the hospital for a few days as she was underweight. As the dream unfolded, she had been walking down the street pushing the twins in a carriage when she met her old high school principal. He crossed the road to greet her.

"I hear you've had twins!" he said. Glancing into the carriage he looked at her with a puzzled expression. "There's only one baby here… where is the other one?"

"She had to stay in the hospital for a few days because she was underweight," she replied.

When indeed she did become pregnant for the second time, she related her dream to the doctor who assured her there was just one fetus. As her pregnancy progressed she'd recount the dream to him again, but he simply scoffed at her, assuring her this was to be a single birth only. One evening while stepping from the shower, she noticed something was askew when she looked into the bathroom mirror to see two distinct bulges protruding from her abdomen. One was high, the other, quite low. Her husband immediately drove her to the hospital where she was informed that she was indeed carrying twins; the birth of one was imminent, but the other twin wasn't ready for delivery. Ordered into the hospital immediately where she was confined for a few weeks, the babies were finally born, and as her dream had predicted, the second one remained in the hospital for a few days longer as she was underweight. And yes, she did run into her old high school principal—their brief conversation mimicking the dream to the word.

A couple of years later, she gave birth to another beautiful son.

Astral projection appeared to be another side effect of her death experiences. Since she could remember, her out-of-body travels were just a normal part of her life. Many times, just prior to falling asleep, there would be a slight ringing in her ears, a prelude to her astral travel. Never frightened during these experiences she rather enjoyed the sights, sounds and foreign places she visited during her numerous astral sprees.

As a child, she presumed everyone traveled outside their bodies, but was soon to realize it was not a common occurrence. In her late twenties she began to explore various theories regarding psychic phenomena—anything that might shed light on her paranormal capabilities. She found the research fascinating, whetting her appetite for a deeper understanding of the unknown, and as a result, she became a parapsychologist, psychotherapist, psychic researcher and "ghostbuster."

Incredulous as the above account seems, I can assure readers that it is one hundred percent accurate. You see...*I was that little girl.*

# INTRODUCTION

*"I say, that of all idiocies, that is most stupid, most vile, and most damnable which holds that after this life there is no other."*

*Dante*

Over the years I have observed the sheer fascination and the countenance of awe on the faces of people to whom I relate various psychic experiences. Hence, the birth of an idea that led to the creation of this book. I truly hope that you derive as much pleasure from reading my book as I have derived from writing it.

As a psychic investigator, lecturer and psychotherapist in the field of parapsychology, counseling on past life regressions and conducting psychic workshops both private and public, I have had the opportunity to meet and become privy to literally hundreds of personalities and their encounters with the paranormal, a portion of which were related to me during private sessions, while others reached my ears via assorted channels. It has been my acute observation that the general population is more than eager to share their bizarre experiences with anyone willing to listen. Though the majority of these individuals were fascinated, even delighted, to have encountered a bona fide psychic experience, others have expressed emotions ranging from slight apprehension to abject terror. The latter category is generally more than eager to broach the subject to me, and with an air likened to that of a religious confession, relate their experiences, anticipating, perhaps, a liberation from the possibility of any further psychic encounters once having divested themselves of their psychically charged preoccupation.

Then there are those who tend to scrutinize their lifestyle in an attempt to detect a rational explanation. They generally believe that the everyday stresses of career and family responsibilities were the root cause of their experience, or perchance (God forbid), that solitary family gene that he or she shares with crazy Aunt Louella has selected to remain latent no longer. In order to alleviate their anxiety and release their ungrounded fears, I acquaint these individuals with the certainty that most everyone, at one time or another during the course of their lives, does indeed experience at least one occurrence—albeit some more dramatic than others—but experience them they do.

There is also a sizeable proportion of the populace I term the "I-wishers." These individuals are so intense in their desire to have a psychic experience that they go to great lengths in order to consciously fabricate yarns designed to impress anyone willing to listen; the extent of the impression resting solely on the degree of expertise the "I-wisher" possesses in the area of imagination. For obvious reasons, it is fortunate that this category is minimal, and that generally most people do accept, as a part of life, the reality of that which we cannot fully comprehend.

"If doubt," as someone once remarked, "is the beginning of wisdom," then "skepticism," as Emerson declared, "is slow intellectual suicide." I firmly adhere to keeping an open mind, for to close your mind in any direction is to stifle your metaphysical growth, which creates "tunnel vision," a most unnatural—not to mention boring—state of mind. Personally, I find my doubt has always acted as a catalyst, impelling me to acquire more knowledge in my chosen field as a psychic researcher.

Another observation I have made during my career as a psychic researcher is that a handful of people are loathe to convey their psychic experiences, not to mention adamantly deny that they have any interest in the subject itself. As Marie Corelli, world-famous English novelist of the 19th century, wrote in *The Life Everlasting:*

"The very idea that any one creature should be fortunate enough to secure some particular advantage which others, through their indolence or indifference, have missed, is sufficient to excite the envy of the weak or the anger of the ignorant. It is impossible that an outsider should enter into a clear understanding of the mystical spiritual-nature world around him and it follows that the teachings and tenets of that spiritual-nature world must be more or less a closed book to such a one—a book, moreover, which he seldom cares or dares to try and open. For this reason the sages concealed much of their profound knowledge from the multitude because they rightly recognized the limitations of narrow minds and prejudiced opinions…What the fool cannot learn he laughs at, thinking that by his laughter he shows superiority instead of latent idiocy."

I have had the pleasure of counseling people from all walks of life—from housewives to the most highly respected professionals and high profile personalities. I know for a fact that the interest in psychic phenomena does not wane according to the amount of formal education and intellectual enlightenment of the individual, as opposed to the belief that only those who are superstitious or ignorant would believe in the supernatural. Interestingly enough, those with a college education are slightly more likely to acknowledge the reality of psychic phenomena than those with less education—60% to 54% to be exact.

Religion also plays a significant role in people's opinions about psychic phenomena. Two-thirds of those who identify themselves as Catholic believe that psychic phenomena occur, whereas only 52% of Protestants and other religions believe it. Strangely enough, there are a number of individuals who boast of at least one bible in their homes, yet they are of the belief that any hint of the supernatural is the work of the devil. Is the bible not filled with accounts of pre-cognitive dreams, clairvoyance, clairaudience and apparitions? For example, what are prayers if not telepathy? And did Jesus not say in St. Matthew 18.20, "For where two or three are gathered together in my name, there am I in the midst of them?"

According to a CBC news poll conducted in 2002, though an equal number of males and females believe in psychic phenomena (57%), 20% of women have experienced it in some form as opposed to just 13% of males. Age seems to be another factor as well. 21% of individuals between the ages of 45 to 64 are most likely to have had a psychic encounter, whereas just 11% under the age of 30 are likely to have had one. Also, 26% of adults who believe in psychic phenomena are more likely to admit to have experienced them, whereas only 4% of non-believers admitted to having experienced such phenomena.

Then there are the (shall we say) "pillars of society" who refuse to even discuss the subject. To cite an example, I have met a number of extremely intelligent professionals who, in their broad ignorance, were swift to decline offering an opinion on the subject of psychic phenomena, whether negative or positive. Needless to say, these personalities were either agnostic (unbelievers in the absolute reality of knowledge) or atheistic (Godless); therefore, if confronted with a psychic experience, they'd fail to recognize it for what it was or, and more importantly, if they were aware of it, they'd be most hesitant to mention the incident to anyone for fear of losing their social status. On the contrary, the most intelligent personalities down through history have more often than not been avid believers in the supernatural.

Einstein, who (and I think the reader will agree with me on this point) had the edge on intelligence) said, "I don't believe that God plays dice with the universe," thereby implying that he was neither Godless nor an unbeliever in the reality of knowledge. He proved that time is not static but linear; therefore, there is no such thing as Time as we know it. One would assume that the more gifted people (in the area of intelligence) would at least realize that the possibility of precognition (supernormal knowledge of impending events) and retrocognition (supernormally acquired knowledge of the past) is a reality.

A firm believer in the continuity of life, Einstein shared his views with Charles Dickens, Abraham Lincoln (who had a precognitive dream of his own funeral down to the last detail), General George Patton (a firm believer in reincarnation), Robert L. Stevenson (who wrote "Kubla Khan" from a dream he'd had the previous night, Freud (the father of psychology) and Carl Jung, his disciple, psychiatrist and parapsychologist. According to Jung, dream symbols that exist in the very depths of the soul behave as if the psychic life of the individual will continue.

It's still hard to believe that as late as the 1920's the majority of scientists were so apprehensive about dealing with any type of psychic research as the field was so disrespected. So disrespected, in fact, that one university psychologist stated that he would not even keep the *Journal of the Society for Psychical Research* in the library for fear that it would inflame the imaginations and corrupt the minds of students.

# ONE

## Poltergeists, Apparitions & Ghosts

As a psychic researcher I have been called upon to investigate the numerous disturbances occurring in some of the most historic architectural structures in Toronto, such as the old City Hall on Queen Street. Built in the 1890's, the structure has been the source of unexplained occurrences throughout the years: tales of judges' robes being tugged as they climb the stairs; cries emanating from the basement that served as a holding center for prisoners; disturbances in the attic and last, but far from least, Courtroom 33 where the last men in Canada were condemned to hang. In his book, *Haunted Toronto*, John Robert Colombo writes of two reporters who, following the Halloween tradition of someone in the Press spending the night at the Old City Hall, only lasted until four in the morning. The uncanny noises and "cool fogs" were a little more than they could bear.

From the moment I set foot in the building, I was surrounded by an almost overwhelming sense of anguish. How many innocent individuals had been unjustly incarcerated or, worse still, sentenced to death in that building we'll never know, but there is no doubt whatsoever that such events did occur, and had I been one undeservedly hung, I'd be yanking on the judge's robes too!

The reader might retort: *There have numerous crimes committed against the innocent, yet there are no reports of hauntings from those scenes.*

True, but there is a significant difference here. The roof of the old Toronto City Hall was copper, and copper retains memory. One could liken this to the art of psychometry, wherein it is possible to obtain paranormal knowledge by using a physical object as a focus. Also known as "object reading" some psychics are able to obtain information such as the true character and surroundings of another individual, be they deceased or alive, simply by focusing on any small object such as a watch, bracelet or ring.

American scientist and physician, J. Rhodes Buchanan, who devoted a great part of his life to exploring the variables of psychic phenomena, coined the term "psychometric" in 1842. He constructed the term "psychometry" from the Greek word "psyche" meaning "soul" and "metron" meaning "measure"; therefore, the literal translation would be "soul measuring." An object regularly worn or used by just one individual is important—particularly a watch, ring or other jewelry worn almost daily.

For example, during a workshop I was giving on psychometry, I grasped in the palm of my hand a ring that had been worn by one of the participants for a number of years. Visions of a small child tossing books away swept through my mind. I related this to the owner of the ring only to hear that her young son had been dismissed from three schools due to his inability and complete disinterest in school. Authorities have declared that one man in every ten, and four women in every ten, are possessed of the innate ability to perform psychometry. In terms of the old Toronto City Hall's copper roof, a dwelling need not have a metal roof in order to retain memories; but due to the extent of the mental anguish experienced by numerous prisoners, combined with the copper roof, it's definitely far more powerful and ineradicable.

## THE MACKENZIE HOUSE

Another building I was called in to investigate is the "MacKenzie House," former residence of Toronto's first Mayor, William Lyon MacKenzie. Without question one of the most infamous structures in Ontario (if not Canada) as a result of the number of reported hauntings, the middle-class Georgian home is located at 82 Bond Street in downtown Toronto, and was a gift to MacKenzie in 1859 from his friends, family and supporters following his ten year exile in the United States. He only resided there for two years until he passed away in his bedroom, situated on the second floor of the house, in 1861. Born in 1795, MacKenzie was leader of the failed 1837 Upper Canada Rebellion of which he was convicted of high treason. As well, he published the most important newspaper of the day known as "The Colonial Advocate." He was also the grandfather of Canada's tenth Prime Minister, W.L. MacKenzie King, (1921 to 1948).

The haunting of MacKenzie's former three-story brick residence began sometime between 1956 and 1966 when one of the caretakers, employed by the city of Toronto and living on the third floor of the house, sighted a frock-coated man. It should be noted the man he saw was bald, and since it is common knowledge that MacKenzie sported a wig to hide his baldness, it was immediately assumed the ghost was that of MacKenzie himself. Oddly enough, it appears that the ghost in question seems to have an obsession with the indoor plumbing—a luxury he didn't have in the house previously.

Other sightings include: a long-haired woman in period dress on the second and third floor; an apparition of a "gray lady" who reportedly slapped a caretaker's wife leaving welts on her face; phantom voices, and footsteps on the stairs. The antique piano in the parlor suddenly began to play at various hours of the day or night, and the ancient printing press once belonging to MacKenzie that was on display in the basement commenced working in the middle of the night.

In July, 2004, the ParaResearchers of Ontario received an email from a witness to an unusual event at Mackenzie House. The name and the personal information of the witness have been removed for their privacy.

I have seen the "lady" up close and she scared me so much that I couldn't walk up darkened stairs for most of my life. I am now twenty-nine, and my sighting took place when I was nine years old, in December of 1983. She appeared old, had long hair and seemed to be hanging suspended on the landing of the stairs as I looked up from the front hallway. She looked right into my eyes and I screamed so loud the staff and my mother and sister came running. I went back one more time with a school trip the following year, and all of my friends worried that it might happen again. Of course, it didn't. I'm not too sure why ghosts appear or why they appear to whom they do, but I would take a lie detector to prove this occurrence actually happened to me. I have had two other occurrences since in other locations, but nothing as scary as seeing a full figure, see-through white woman looking right through me. I hope this has convinced someone; I know my friends and family members are too scared to even visit the house. I cannot be certain of what era the "apparition" I saw came from, but I do remember the clothing appearing to be of another century, perhaps the 18th century. She wore a long dress with a lot of ruffles, from what I can recall. I have no idea if she was related to MacKenzie, but I would guess her costume was from over 100 years ago, at the very least. I can still somewhat see her in my mind, even though I've tried to forget. I guess I just really want people out there to know what I saw, and I wonder if others have witnessed the same sight as myself.

Upon my arrival in the home, I found nothing disquieting; however, I was drawn to the parlor where the impression of a young woman playing the piano was perceptible to me. I repeated the necessary prayers in order to release any earthbound souls and from what I understand, there have been no signs of hauntings since my visit.

## ALCATRAZ PRISON

Without question, the most disturbed building I've ever set foot in was Alcatraz Prison, home to the infamous Al Capone for many years. Originally a prison and an Army fort, the prison was converted to a jail in 1934. Literally impossible to escape from, the conditions within were nothing short of appalling. Prisoners, forbidden to talk at all, murdered each other, mutilated themselves and committed suicide on a daily basis, or went completely insane. Beaten constantly by the guards, their terrifying screams echoed throughout the prison day and night; screams that can still be heard, particularly from the dungeon.

Many tourists visiting the prison feel extremely weird in the area of "14-D" where the temperature is freezing although the day may be extremely hot. Since the closing of the prison, tourist guides (and some visitors) reported sounds of screaming, running feet, the clanging of metal doors and horrifying shrieks reverberating from the dungeon. There have also been numerous reports of banjo music emanating from the shower room once utilized by Al Capone.

A former guard of the prison tells of his experiences regarding Cell Block D (particularly cells 12 and 14) and the frightening energy lingering in the cavernous portion of the prison. During the 1940's convicts were often confined in one of the 14 cells in "D" block. Cells 9-14 were called "The Hole" because they didn't have any windows, and only one light that could be turned off by the guards. The darkness gave the impression they were in a hole in the ground—hence the name.

On one occasion an inmate was locked up in "The Hole." Within a matter of seconds the inmate began screaming and yelling that there was someone with glowing eyes in there with him. There had been rumors of a ghostly presence wandering the darkened corridors wearing clothing of the 1800's, and since the rumors were a continual source of practical joking among the guards, the inmate's screaming was simply ignored. He continued screaming well into the night, until there was silence. When a guard inspected the cell the following day, he found the convict dead, a terrible expression on his face and noticeable hand marks around his throat. An autopsy revealed that the strangulation was definitely not self-inflicted, though some argued that a guard who had tired of his constant screaming had strangled him. Others, however, believe it was the restless, evil spirit of a former inmate who exacted his vengeance on the helpless inmate.

Adding to the mystery, the day after the tragedy, several guards, performing a routine lineup of the convicts, counted one too many men. At the end of the line the guards saw an extra body—that of the recently deceased convict. As everyone stared at him in utter disbelief, the figure of the ghostly presence simply vanished into thin air!

We began to find the first authenticated ghost stories towards the end of the eighteenth century. One early example, set in 1774 during the War of Independence, revolves around a spirit that was "heard, but not seen," to quote the title of a contemporary account. It seems that two British officers were awaiting the return of a Major Bloomberg who was out on a foraging party. Eventually, their patience all but exhausted, they heard his familiar footsteps approaching the outside of the tent. However, instead of entering, the Major seemed to pause outside. A voice then addressed the men instructing one of them that, when he returned home to England he was to go to a certain house in Westminster and there, in a room which the voice minutely described, he would find papers of great interest and importance to the Major's ten-year-old son. The footsteps then turned and faded away in the distance.

Puzzled by their friend's behavior, the two soldiers rushed out of the tent—but there was no sign of the Major. A guard on duty was questioned, but insisted he had neither seen nor heard anyone. As they stood talking, a party emerged from the woods carrying a man's corpse. It was that of Major Bloomberg, who had been killed about ten minutes earlier. Three bullets causing instant death had struck the body, and it could only be concluded that the Major had addressed his friends in one place at the very time of his death in another.

This bizarre story doesn't end there—for on his return to England, the friend searched the house in Westminster and found deeds to property in Yorkshire, which the Major had hidden away as an inheritance for his son. The event became the topic of much society gossip on both sides of the Atlantic; Queen Charlotte herself was so intrigued by it that she had the young Bloomberg brought up in the Royal Nursery and employed Gainsborough to paint his portrait as a memorial to the phantom who was "heard, but not seen."

According to Peter Haining, author of *Ghosts: The Illustrated History* (1987) a census carried out by the Society for Psychical Research (SPR) at the turn of the twentieth century indicated that approximately one person in sixteen saw or heard a ghost during his or her lifetime. This extraordinarily high figure was arrived at by the modern method of taking a cross-section of the public: Some 17,000 people were canvassed, of whom 1,684 said they had had some form of supernatural experience. As with all such calculations, this result (nearly 10%) should be treated with caution; yet, just as the latest political-opinion poll can give us an indication of public attitudes, so can the "ghost-poll" highlight modern man's receptiveness to supernatural phenomena. Not everyone may believe in ghosts, but that a large proportion of the population is prepared to treat the subject seriously is clearly evident.

One of the myths surrounding ghosts is that they are only seen at night; however, their appearance is not restricted to the small hours of night or times of seclusion. They can appear at the most unexpected moments, appearing in public as well. For example, a ghost in evening dress was seen one morning in a London street in 1878. The *Daily Telegraph* reported that "a woman fled in affright; the figure had a most cadaverous look, but the next person the apparition encountered recognized it as that of a friend, a foreigner." This next person was Dr. Armand Leslie. His friend was found dead in evening clothes in a foreign city at the time his phantasm was seen. However, occurences like this are very rare.

At the beginning of the new century, too, enquiry into all aspects of the occult was progressing more earnestly than ever, and throughout the western world new research organizations and societies burgeoned. Individuals were also exploring the various realms of the supernatural, and these years saw the publication of some of the most scholarly— often the definitive—works on topics like witchcraft, mysticism and ghosts. For the first time in centuries writers had gone back to the original source material rather than rewriting earlier books; consequently, much new speculation and alteration of opinion occurred.

This trend has continued unabated to the present time when we are now questioning our very origins and even discussing the possibility that many of our ancient legends may reflect the visits to this planet of extra-terrestrial beings. According to the Oxford English Dictionary, a ghost is the spirit or immaterial part of a man as distinct from the body, and is spoken of as appearing in visible form or otherwise manifesting itself to the living. The word itself is derived from the Saxon "gaste" or "gest," and in the north of England the term "guest" is still occasionally used to describe an apparition.

To this very day, Christianity has continued to acknowledge the possibility of ghosts and spirits. The exorcism ceremony is still used for driving out harmful spirits and for combating devils. A case in point is that of the famous Christian ascetic, St. Anthony, who lived much of his life in abstinence and devotion, and is regarded as the founder of

Christian monasticism. Allegedly, he had numerous encounters with demons and ghosts. Doubtless, St. Anthony's extensive fasting may have been in part responsible for both the apparitions and the *filthy, maddening thoughts* which plagued him. It has recently been suggested that he may have eaten bread infected with the fungus, *Claviceps purpurea*, which contains lysergic acid, the natural source of L.S.D., and that this would account for his many "visions"; nonetheless, his struggles with phantoms have provided a rich source of inspiration for painters, several of whom have given much attention to the beautiful female ghost which allegedly attempted to lure him into carnal pleasures.

## POLTERGEISTS, APPARITIONS OR GHOSTS?

Ghosts can be variously "classified" for easy identification. First, there is the ghost that returns to haunt the earth without harm to man, often bringing messages or warnings to the living. Then, there is the "poltergeist," a destructive, noisy and impish spirit that tends to throw objects, make strange noises, pull the covers off sleeping individuals and has been known to sexually attack young women. Then, there is the "fetch" or "double" of a living person that is about to die. There is also the spectral animal or creature—not to mention the occasional inanimate object such as a the "phantom ship," which usually haunts lonely wastes.

The North American Indians have, since time immemorial, revered spirits. Their "Ghost Dance" in honour of the dead is one of the most colourful and exciting ceremonies in the world. There is a saying among the Algonquin Indians that "the shadow souls of the dead chirp like crickets."

Experts who have studied the phenomenon have established what they consider to be five basic explanations for the appearances of ghosts:

1. The theory of reincarnation tells us we have lived previous lives and that ghosts are simply reincarnations (dressed in garments

of the period) of those individuals half-consciously remembered from former lives.

2. They are the result of extreme mental conflict which has "imprinted a photograph" on the astral light, which anyone with the slightest glimmer of psychic faculty is able to perceive.

3. That we actually do see ghosts—dead people who are capable of rebuilding their bodily forms, however unsubstantially, and thereby revisiting the scenes in which they spent their lives.

4. That they are hybrid beings created by the disembodied spirit of a deceased person combining with some substance to produce a temporary, albeit extremely primitive, intelligence.

5. That they are created out of the universal fascination and fear of ghosts by static memory and dynamic consciousness—that is, a layer of consciousness superimposed upon a mechanism of memory.

Ghosts appear in many forms as well as displaying diverse behaviors. For example:

## POLTERGEIST

The term "poltergeist," is derived from the German terms, "poltern," "to knock," and "geist," meaning," spirit or "noisy ghost." The poltergeist makes its presence known by making noises, shrieking, moving objects from one place to another, slamming doors, opening and shutting windows, and on occasion, assaulting people and animals. Interference with electronic equipment including telephones, lights and appliances is also common. They often bring with them a foul smell and there are many reports of agents being bitten, hit or even sexually attacked. Poltergeist activities have been reported in many countries, and chronicled by occult writers such as A. R. G. Owen and Colin Wilson.

The "Epworth Poltergeist" case is one of the best-documented cases of poltergeist activity and was officially recorded in 1716 at the Parsonage in Epworth, Lincolnshire. For two months the Wesley family were bombarded with loud, uncanny noises and rappings. According to the specific notes kept by Mrs. Wesley, she and her husband were descending the stairs one day when they heard a noise as if someone was emptying a large bag of coins at their feet, followed by the sound of glass bottles being "dashed to a thousand pieces." Though some cases of poltergeist activity remain unsolved, scientific investigation has proved that such phenomena can be humanly activated by subconscious psychokinesis brought on by repressed anger, hostility and sexual tension.

William Roll, project director of the Psychical Research Foundation in Durham, North Carolina, explored the theory of living beings sparking off poltergeist activity by studying 116 written reports of cases spanning over four centuries in more than one hundred countries. Roll coined the term "recurrent spontaneous psychokinesis" or (RSPK), meaning inexplicable, spontaneous physical effects. He found that the most common agent was a young adult whose unknowing PK was a great way to express their built-up hostility without fear of punishment. Though unaware of the source of the turmoil, they were, nevertheless, secretly pleased that they transpired.

Recorded since ancient times, poltergeist activity was analyzed in the late 1970's by parapsychologists, Ian Gauld and A. D. Cornell. A computer analysis of cases collected from as far back as 1800 enabled them to identify sixty-three general characteristics of poltergeist activity: 67 percent involved the movement of small objects; 58 percent were more active at night; 48 percent featured raps; 36 percent involved movement of large objects, 24 percent lasted for more than a year; 16 percent involved communication and 12 percent involved the closing and opening of doors.

Some psychic investigators have determined that agents who suffer from poor mental health or who are attempting to deal with unresolved emotional tensions are more likely to be associated with houses where poltergeist activity occurs. In a study dealing with the personalities of agents, psychologists have determined that anxiety reactions, phobias, obsessions, mania, schizophrenia are not uncommon. In some cases, however, the poltergeist activity was eliminated following the agent's therapy. The development and continued research during the late 19th and early 20th centuries validate the authenticity of poltergeist activity. Among the initial investigators were two founders of the Society for Psychical Research (SPR), Sir William Barrett and Frederick H. Meyers. Meyers believed in the genuiness of poltergeist activity and that they differed from ghost hauntings. Parapsychologist Dr. Ian Stevenson proposes that spirits of the dead can quite possibly be the source of poltergeist activity more often than most of us realize. He has investigated numerous cases attributed to spirits of the dead as well as agents and concluded there is a significant difference; for example, the poltergeist phenomena in living cases that were violent occurred for no specific reason, while cases involving spirits of the deceased included intelligent communication and very little violence.

Poltergeist phenomena may also be produced by subconscious psychokinesis on the part of an individual. (Psychokinesis is the paranormal influence of the mind on physical events and processes.) As a rule, poltergeist activity begins and ends abruptly, the duration lasting from several hours to several months; however, a number of cases have extended over a number of years. The disturbances generally begin at night when there is someone present. Generally, this "someone" is the agent, an individual who, for one reason or another, appears to serve as the target for the activity. The agent is generally female under the age of twenty.

In the 1930's, parapsychologist and psychologist, Nandor Fodor, advanced the theory that some poltergeist activity was not caused by spirits but rather by human agents suffering from intense hostility, repressed anger and sexual tension. Furthermore, Fodor was successful in demonstrating his theory in several cases, including the famous "Thornton Heath Poltergeist" in England, which he investigated in 1938. The case involved a woman whose repressions caused a poltergeist outbreak, and apparently, a vampire attack.

In 1721, the renowned Oriental scholar, Professor Shupart, was subjected to the wrath of a poltergeist in his home at Groben. The spirit hurled household objects throughout the house, some weighing more than ten pounds! The professor was unable to sleep in his bed for over a month and wouldn't even undress in the room. His wife was also bitten, pinched and knocked down several times by the spirit. Several groups of people were invited to the home by Shupart to witness the extraordinary events, and on one occasion, no fewer than twelve witnesses saw a violent attack on the Professor by invisible hands.

By far the most fascinating case of poltergeist activity I've yet to come across is the disturbances that have occurred in the home of Mrs. Inca Ceolin. Following the demise of her husband, Inca and her mother-in-law shared the home until failing health required the older woman to enter a nursing home. Discontented with the move, she cursed her daughter-in-law. Shortly thereafter, Inca's cat, Toby, began to charge at something in the home that was visible to him only. He would stand on his hind legs and, as Inca tells it, "shadow box." Every evening around ten o'clock, the front door would begin to shake and rattle for no reason. The cat never ran to the door, choosing instead to sit and stare until the rattling ceased. Only then would he approach the area and begin sniffing at the mysterious door. The house began to fill with a strange mist and closed doors would open by themselves.

One evening while preparing to take her shower, Inca went to the linen closet to retrieve her favorite nightgown, which always hung in the same place. It wasn't there. Puzzled, she searched the other closets, her drawers and the laundry basket. Unable to find it, she chose another gown to wear. Following her shower, she went downstairs, sat on the couch and watched television for a while before going to bed. The next morning, she came downstairs only to find her favorite nightgown laid out neatly on the couch. The radio on Inca's night table was always set to the same station, as was the radio in her car. Upon awakening one morning she turned the radio on only to find the station had been changed. The same thing happened in her car, albeit with a slight difference. The interior of the car reeked with the scent of cigarette smoke, even though it was literally impossible for anyone to get inside the garage where the car was parked.

One evening, while resting in her living room, she was startled by the sudden movement of the couch upon which she sat. It was, in her words, "like someone had shoved the couch from behind." As if that weren't enough, while lying in bed one evening, the same thing happened. She got up and searched the bedroom for any clues as to what had happened, but everything was exactly as it should be.

An extremely clean woman, Inca was horrified one morning upon finding strange footprints on her bathroom mat. She was shocked to see that the shower door had been opened. Not long after, a distinct ring appeared around the tub. Upon entering the bathroom one evening, Inca was shocked to feel someone or something grab her by the shoulder. Even more disturbing, she awoke one morning to find a bleeding cut on her finger. She put a bandage on her finger, but was shocked the following morning when removing it to clean her finger—there was no cut! It had completely disappeared! Since poltergeists are reputed to have a penchant for cutting or slashing their preferred victims, Inca was in for another bout soon after.

One evening she was slicing some tofu on the cutting board in her kitchen when the doorbell rang. Placing the knife on the cutting board, she left the room to answer the door. When she returned she noticed splashes of water covering the window above her kitchen sink. Although she had placed a few dishes in the sink for washing, she hadn't put in the soap or water yet. Pondering as to what might have caused the water on the window, she filled the sink with soap and water, preparing to do the dishes. As she placed her hands into the hot soapy water, a sharp pain in one of her fingers prompted her to remove her hand from the sink only to find the finger bleeding profusely. She couldn't understand it as she hadn't placed anything sharp in the sink. Draining the water out she was able to find, lying at the bottom of the sink, the knife that had been left on the cutting board! Once again, the following day, after removing the bandage, there was absolutely no evidence of a cut!

Feathers began appearing in her bathroom as well as in her bed, and pieces of glass were scattered on the carpet in her basement. The flower vase and lace doily gracing her dining room table were found on the floor one morning. Orbs began to materialize on her door at about the same time she distinctly felt someone grab her by the ankle.

Yet another unexplained incident occurred at a time when she was confined to her bed during a severe bout of pneumonia. One of her friends dropped by the house to see if she could be of any help. As they were chatting, a loud crash resounded from the kitchen. Her friend rushed in to investigate only to find an empty bottle of wine vinegar sitting near the sink, its contents poured all over the surface of the counter, on the floor, and in the sink. Even more frightening was the fact that the vinegar bottle, which was full, had been in the refrigerator just a few minutes previously. There was no one else in the house at the time!

On several occasions, upon unlocking her car in the garage, she was shocked to find scattered on the seats, money, hair, chewing gum, and cigarettes. The light in her garage began turning on and off mysteriously at all hours and loud crashing sounds emanated from her kitchen and laundry room. A large blast in the house awoke her in the middle of the night, yet there was no evidence of any damage. One evening she ran to the basement following a crashing sound only to find her furnace door lying on the floor!

# APPARITIONS

## Deathbed Visions

Nobel prize winner, Professor Charles Richet, who took a deep interest in psychical research, was most impressed by deathbed visions. Professor Karlis Osis has done great work in collecting accounts from doctors and nurses on this phenomenon. Patients, whose last hour has struck, have been reported seeing visions of near relatives appearing at their bedside. They have been seen focusing their attention on a point in space where they see the apparition. In rare cases, people present in the room see the apparition as well, feel an unexplainable cold draught, hear a rushing sound, or see some kind of curious luminosity. Other visitors may partake in the resulting exaltation.

Not only terminal patients see such visions. In fact, one of the first research projects of the SPR in 1889 was to collect accounts of people seeing apparitions. The question asked was: *Have you ever, when believing yourself completely awake, had a vivid impression of seeing or being touched by a living being or an inanimate object or of hearing a voice; which impression was not due to any external physical cause?*

In this "Census of Hallucinations" some 17,000 cases were being studied and the most trustworthy were published. It was ascertained that about ten percent of the population had such an experience. The conclusion was that there must be some connection between the death of a person and an apparition. Sometimes the phantasm of a deceased person seems to come for the sole purpose of conveying urgent information to the surviving relative. In one of such cases the late farmer, James Chaffin, appeared to his son to show him that he had hidden his last Will in his Bible.

Many cases have been documented of people being forewarned of a coming disaster by an apparition. In other cases apparitions, sometimes seen as angels, gave life-saving advice. This was certainly the case in the wonderful story shared by Sidona:

In May of 2003, I spent some time volunteering in Guatamala. I also volunteer in the Palliative Care unit of the local hospital. During this time I met and befriended a palliative patient whom I will call Peter. I spent time with Peter for over a year in the Palliative Care Unit, the Continuing Care Unit and three times a week in the Dialysis Unit. Peter was eighty-two and in extremely poor health; he was not ever expected to leave the Palliative Care Unit. Our relationship started as one of volunteer and patient and ended as two people who loved and cared for each other. Peter was strongly supportive of my volunteer work and encouraged me to travel to Guatemala. Peter died just before I left.

Near the end of my stay in Guatemala I experienced something with Peter that has moved me spiritually and changed my life in many positive ways. I had become quite ill during the end of my stay in Guatamala. For a few days I experienced severe chills with a low-grade fever and it was looking like I had possibly contracted malaria. My condition stayed the same for three or four days and I was becoming weaker and weaker, and in all honesty, more frightened. Being in a third world country that is in a state of anarchy with no proper health care or a quick way out can create a severe sense of unease when you are as ill and weak as I was.

About the fourth night of lying in bed very chilled I truly felt as though I was never going to live through whatever illness I had contracted. I had become so cold that it was impossible to get warm. I lay awake in the dark because electricity is very scarce and even turning on the light was frowned upon. I don't know how many hours went by, but I was not winning and I knew I was becoming sicker. Suddenly, I felt very calm. All the fear seemed to be draining from my body and I can tell you that for a moment I thought I might have died; however, I felt warm and I could hear Peter's voice. He was telling me that everything was going to be okay and that I just needed to hold on a little longer. My eyes were open and I could see him and he was holding me; but it was his upper body and his arms were wings. I know how this sounds, but he had his wings wrapped around me, and the warmth and comfort that he gave me that night truly saved my life.

The following morning, although I was not fully recovered, I felt well enough to get up and make arrangements to go home. Peter had always said that he would always be there for me, and in fact, the Christmas before he died he had sent me a card that said, *Thank You So Much For Your Caring This Past Year, You Won't Be Forgotten, Love, Peter.*

This experience is one I have pondered many times and for a long time after I returned home I did not repeat it to anyone. I am able to talk about it now although it isn't easy. Peter was a very special man and I feel truly blessed to ever have known him.

Apparitions have been observed to cast a shadow, be reflected in a mirror, overturn furniture, make sounds while walking, leave a scent, ask for a lift, in short, demonstrate to possess an active intelligence.

An apparition experience is awareness of the presence of a personal being whose physical body is not in the area of the experiencer, provided the experiencer is sane and in a normal waking state of consciousness. In contrast to extrasensory perception (ESP) of a distant event, the apparition is felt to be in the immediate vicinity of the experiencer. Though an apparition might appear so lifelike as to be mistaken for a real, live person, its rapid disappearance verifies its ghostliness. Generally, the apparitions are someone who is deceased, but there have been reports of individuals still living as well as complete strangers appearing to the viewer. More often than not the apparition disappears within a minute or so. As well, the apparition is able to move easily through walls, cast shadows and their reflection can be seen in mirrors. They sometimes appear to be real and at other times appear either transparent or extremely fuzzy. It is not unusual for an apparition to give the onlooker the sensation of chills accompanied by smells; for example, that of sulfur. The majority of apparitions appear to have a purpose, such as communicating a message.

Most interesting are the "collective" apparitions in which more than one person can see the apparition. Animals are aware of apparitions and the sight of one will cause cats to bristle and dogs to whine or bark. Apparitions are also able to perform activities such as turning lights off and on as well as opening locked doors. The sound of footsteps can often be heard as well when there is an apparition in the near vicinity.

Then there are the "deathbed" apparitions wherein angelic-type beings appear to comfort the dying. Then there are the individuals who, at the point of death, wish to bid farewell to a loved one who lives far away. Just before death or a short time afterwards, their spirit will appear to the loved one, ever so briefly, before dissipating. As mentioned, this phenomenon happened to me a few times, and speaking for myself, I found the experience rather comforting and not the least bit menacing.

Methods for researching apparition experiences were largely developed by the SPR and have now reached a high level of efficiency. Modern advances in psychology, psychiatry, sociology, and forensic sciences are incorporated, as well as techniques of qualitative and quantitative investigation. Mere hallucinations, hypnagogic and hypnopompic imagery, mistaken identity, illusory reshaping of normal stimuli, deliberate hoaxes, and chance coincidences have had to be identified and sifted off in the process of serious research. Journalistic books usually bypass methodological rigor and can be misleading as to actual observations.

Apparitions are experienced in many ways. "Seeing" is the most frequent sense modality that furnishes this experience. The apparition might look so lifelike that it is mistaken for a flesh-and-bones person. Only sudden vanishing gives away its ghostly nature. Sometimes, however, the images represent only parts of the body, or appear as vague and misty outlines. They might portray the dead, the living, or unidentifiable strangers. Sounds, such as steps approaching and doors opening, are often heard. Touch, smell, and temperature sensations may be reported, but sometimes the experience is of a "felt presence" without any specific sensory qualities. Apparitions usually are of short duration; less than a minute. They can be a once-in-a-lifetime experience, or recurrent.

Not all apparitions are of interest for the afterlife issue. Many have been traced to various different roots. Some were thought to be hallucinations, the cognitive content of which was derived from a telepathic message that is then projected out like a mental slide, from "retrocognition," or the sudden glance of events in a time long past; for example, D-Day in Normandy, or a scene from Marie Antoinette's time. If a mother sees her son walking through the kitchen with drenched clothes at the time he was drowned, that experience could hardly be separable from her own ESP projection of her son's image in the kitchen. But if neighbors see him entering the kitchen door at the same time, that would be of interest.

ESP, like our other thoughts and feelings, is a private experience that is directly observable only by the experiencer. Some apparition phenomena, however, have been collectively experienced by several persons; about one-third of those apparition experiences where more than one person was present, awake, and in a position to see, were collective (Hornell Hart, 1959). Often, animals also react: dogs growl, cats bristle. In haunted houses, phenomena may be reported as occurring repeatedly over the years to the distress of the family and the surprise of visitors. For example, in a house near Pittsburgh, sixteen witnesses have reported observations of some ghostly phenomena over a period of twenty years. The exact nature of stimuli in collective cases is still unknown, but apparitions that are collectively seen do suggest a disembodied agency. Numerous attempts have been made to explain them, such as by the super-ESP hypothesis. However, these explanations have been severely criticized (Alan Gauld, 1977, 1982), because ESP of the magnitude and reliability needed to account for the observed phenomena has not been found.

Usually, an apparition appears to perform physical actions, such as opening doors, but nothing is later found to have been moved. The noises of opening and closing doors turn out to be an imitation of the sounds of real events. On rare occasions, however, physical objects are affected: lights or gadgets are switched on or off, locked doors are reported opening, and so on. L.E. Rhine (1957) advanced an explanation that does not presume a discarnate agency. She claimed that psychic forces (psychokinesis, PK) of the observer could do the same as the ostensible ghost. The formidable burden of this hypothesis is to explain why such a mighty psychokinetic effect occurs at the moment of an apparition experience to people who have never exerted such an effort before or after in their lives.

In two-thirds of poltergeist cases, a living agent has been identified; however, such cases are very rare in comparison with the frequency of reported hauntings and the patterns of both phenomena differ markedly. Poltergeist phenomena are linked to persons who must be present for the effects to occur. Furthermore, the time sequences and movements of objects seem to be different (and much more destructive). Apparition cases that involve physical action are very unnerving to those who investigate because they cannot be readily explained away as hallucinations.

Contradictory to common belief, ghosts (and apparitions) generally haunt places, not people. If a spirit in the 1500's haunted—for whatever reason—a certain geographical area, you can rest assured that he or she still haunts the same area today even though, through the centuries, that one particular area has been occupied by numerous houses or buildings that once existed. Perhaps a skyscraper now occupies the ghost's territory, but chances are the spirit is still there.

To cite an example, I was called in to investigate the elegant home of a prominent Toronto physician who chooses to remain anonymous. Strange phenomena were occurring in his home since the death of his mother who had resided with him and his wife until her demise. Water taps turned on by themselves, lights relit moments after being turned out, but the thing that caused them the greatest concern was the condition of the infant's nursery. No matter how warm the house was kept, the nursery was constantly ice cold. The moment I entered the home, the name of a well-known Canadian corporation kept flashing through my mind. When I mentioned this to the doctor, he informed me that his father-in-law had been employed there for many years before his death a few years previous. He also told me that his mother had suffered from severe arthritis and his new young wife was reluctant to let the older woman hold the newborn for fear she would drop her. Obviously, the grandmother felt terrible about this, but no matter how much she pleaded to hold the infant her requests were denied.

Upon entering the nursery, I saw the spirit of the grandmother leaning over the crib. Her presence in the nursery explained the cold temperature: in order for a ghost to materialize they require heat, generally from a living soul or the surroundings. Naturally, the loss of body heat borrowed from the spirit causes the individual to look paler than normal; hence the expression," You look like you've seen a ghost."

It was obvious to me that the grandmother, even in death, still desired to hold and protect her grandchild and chose to stand vigil by the infant's crib. I said the necessary prayers in order to release the grandmother's spirit from her earthly attachment and there were no future problems in the home after that.

One of the most famous ghosts in history is that of the sixteenth President of the United States—Abraham Lincoln. That the spirit should be his is perhaps expected when one realizes how deeply interested he was in psychic research even to the point where he held serious séances in the White House. Mrs. Eleanor Roosevelt has recorded perhaps the best story of Lincoln's ghost:

> I was sitting in my study when one of the maids burst in on me in a state of great excitement. I looked up from my work and asked her what was the trouble.
>
> "He's up there—sitting on the edge of the bed, taking off his shoes!" she exclaimed.
>
> "Who's up there taking off his shoes?" I asked.
>
> "Mr. Lincoln!" the maid replied.

Queen Wilhelmina of the Netherlands saw the ghost during a state visit. While spending a night at the White House during the Roosevelt presidency, she was awakened by a knock on the bedroom door. Answering it, she was confronted with the ghost of Abe Lincoln staring at her from the hallway. As well, Presidents Theodore Roosevelt, Herbert Hoover and Harry Truman all reported hearing unexplained rappings on their bedroom doors. They all believed it was Lincoln.

It is no secret that Lincoln was more than a little distressed over the Civil War. It appeared that his spirit might have continued worrying long after his death. On several occasions, the wife of Calvin Coolidge reported having seen the ghost of Lincoln standing with his hands clasped behind his back, at a window in the Oval Office, staring out in deep contemplation toward the bloody battlefields across the Potomac.

During one of his visits to the States during World War Two, Winston Churchill spent the night at the White House. As he was wont to do, he retired late, following a long, hot bath while imbibing a glass of Scotch, smoking a cigar and just relaxing. However, on one occasion, he climbed out of the bath and naked, save for his cigar, sauntered into the adjoining bedroom. Startled, he looked up to see Abraham Lincoln standing by the fireplace in the room, leaning on the mantle. Churchill simply blinked before saying, "Good evening, Mr. President. You seem to have me at a disadvantage." Lincoln apparently smiled softly before simply disappearing.

All sightings of Lincoln have ceased since the Truman administration. It is believed to be the result of the numerous renovations to the presidential home. Lincoln's ghost, however, was not confined to the White House. Some have spotted his spirit walking near his gravesite in Springfield, Illinois; while others have claimed to see his ghostly funeral train many years after it carried his body back to Springfield. According to some witnesses, there are two trains seen on the anniversary of that first journey: the first train pulls a line of black-draped cars and the second pulls just one flatbed car on which is the slain president's casket.

It is well documented that Lincoln had a precognitive dream regarding his untimely death. He related his dream to his close friend, Ward Hill Lamon. In Lincoln's words:

> About ten days ago, I retired very late. I soon began to dream. There seemed to be a death-like stillness about me. Then I heard subdued sobs, as if a number of people were weeping. I thought I left my bed and wandered downstairs. There the silence was broken by the same pitiful sobbing, but the mourners were invisible. I went from room to room. No living person was in sight, but the same mournful sounds met me as I passed alone. I was puzzled and alarmed. Determined to find the cause of the state of things so mysterious and shocking, I kept on until I arrived at the East Room. Before me was a catafalque on which rested a corpse wrapped in funereal

vestments. Around it were stationed soldiers who were acting as guard; and there was a throng, or people, some gazing mournfully upon the corpse, whose face was covered. Others were weeping pitifully.

"Who is dead in the White House? I demanded of one of the soldiers."

"The President," was his answer. "He was killed by an assassin."

Harry Truman noted in his diary in 1945: "The maids and butlers swear he has appeared on several occasions." Mr. Truman himself was disturbed by a knocking on his door one night and finding no one there concluded: "I think it must have been Lincoln's ghost walking the hall."

Not only has Lincoln's spirit been seen in the White House halls, but numerous sightings of his spirit meandering about the Lincoln grave in Springfield, Illinois have been reported as well. It is interesting to note that Lincoln's wife, Mary Todd Lincoln, was fascinated with the spiritual world as well, a fascination that increased following the demise of their young son William.

Many people tend to doubt themselves in a situation where they've seen a ghost. Perhaps they tend to blame the sighting on their inferior eyesight or assume their imagination is working overtime. One thing you can be sure of…if there is an animal in the house at that particular time and they become agitated in any way, you can be sure you've seen a bona fide spirit. Animals, particularly cats and dogs, are incredibly psychic. Take the case of Mrs. Lily Caravella from Schomberg, Ontario. She woke in the middle of the night and happened to glance toward the dimly lit bathroom. At the same time that she saw the outline of the top half of a ghost slowly disappearing into the bathroom wall, her dog became excited, and running toward the bathroom continued his barking. If the dog hadn't been present perhaps Mrs. Caravella might have thought her eyes were playing tricks on her as she was still sleepy; but when it became obvious to her that the dog had sighted the spirit as well she knew she had seen a real ghost.

Mrs. Caravella's account of her experience brings to mind a write-up in the "Proceedings of the Society for Psychical Research," Volume VIII. The account is of two dogs confronted by a ghost. One of the dogs, excited and with tail a'wagging, ran to greet it, but upon realizing it was a spirit, ran away terrified. It appears that as humans we are limited somewhat by our senses; for example, there are sounds well beyond our range of hearing that dogs can hear. As well, the canines are able to detect odors that we can't. Certainly cats can see much better in the dark than we can; therefore, it makes sense that although we occupy the same world, these animals are able to see, hear and smell things that are far beyond the reach of our human senses. It is not terribly unusual for a dog to begin whining uncontrollably at the exact moment of it's owner's death even though they may have been hundreds of miles away at the time of their demise.

Dogs and cats are not the only animals that have psychic abilities. Sir William Barrett (1845-1926) was a distinguished psychic researcher who recorded an incident involving two sisters who spotted a ghost drifting across the road on which they were traveling. Their horse stopped immediately and began to tremble with fear.

This is Duo's account of a typical ghostly encounter:

For several years there has been a young girl of roughly seven, who I can only assume is a ghost, that runs frantically into my bedroom at night, rousing me between eleven and midnight. This has happened on several occasions, and though supernatural things normal don't bother me, I was a bit shaken up by her, because unlike other things I'd experienced, she physically shook me awake and whispered my name. Her presence was a frightening one, despite how young she seemed to be.

I decided to sleep in my living room after one of the nightly attacks, and still do to this day, because this seemingly innocent ghost has gotten violent. One morning I woke in my living room and everything was dreadfully cold. I could feel someone in the room, but it wasn't until I heard my name whispered that I became concerned. I could tell it was the girl, but she didn't sound so small and frightened anymore. Actually, she sounded like she was trying to scare me. I became very suspicious that the thing in my house was not a little girl, but something unfriendly that was posing as one.

My suspicions were realized about a month ago. I put my dog outside, and when I went to let him back in I saw an enormous black dog dart through my yard and around the side of my house, which promptly disappeared when I looked to see where it was running to. That night while in the shower, I felt something sting my leg and I looked down to see a large claw mark going up the side of my leg. For a second I thought that my dog must have done it, until I realized how fresh it looked. I finished showering and decided to take a look at the strange claw marks again, but all that I could find on my leg were three small strips of reddish skin where the scratches had been, and a hand print left on my leg much smaller than my own would be. I can only assume, since it was a hand print the size of a child's, that it was the thing that used to wake me up all the time, but I can't make sense of what the big dog had to do with anything.

There have been numerous reports of so-called "Dog Spirits" who, for one reason or another, are wont to remain in this world. Take, for example, the story of Chris S. and her encounter with one:

In 1990 I was living in my grandmother-in-law's house. I had just given birth to my second child and was staying in a bedroom in her house that used to be occupied by my father-in-law when he was a boy. My grandmother-in-law's name was Virginia and she had lived in the house since the 1950's with her husband and a pet dog named Peanut. Peanut was a small cocker spaniel and was the family pet for fifteen years before passing away. The floors of the house were all wooden and there was a long hallway that led to all of the bedrooms.

One night I woke up to hear a clicking sound outside in the hallway. It sounded as if something was moving up and down the hall in a run, like an animal with its nails clicking along the wooden floors and echoing in the hallway. I first thought it was Virginia's cats playing in the hall at night. After this, the same phenomenon happened at least four or five more times. I asked Virginia about it and what the sound was. She said it was probably the dog, Peanut, because the cats were never in at night and would not make such a loud clicking sound in the hall with their nails. I said "oh" and went about my business. Now, I always had my door shut and sometimes locked at night, especially after hearing about this *ghost dog*.

One night I woke up to hear Peanut running up and down the hall once again, and I cringed under my covers listening to him run. Then all of the sudden I heard him stop. Just then I felt as if something had jumped onto my bed and had lain down upon my feet on the bed. I froze. I didn't breathe. I didn't even look out of my covers. I lay like this for about two to three minutes. I did reach out though to feel at my feet on top of the covers. Just as I reached out and touched my feet, the sensation of a heavy thing lying on my feet went away.

That was the only time Peanut came to sleep on my bed, but I did hear him running up and down the hall many more times during the six months I lived there. Since then I am sure there are lingering spirits or energies.

Visits from deceased loved ones are far more common than the general public is aware of, simply because we are far closer to them whilst in the sleeping state, a state that permits our sixth sense the liberty to explore the higher realms. While sleeping, we've crossed the dividing line between physical and spiritual. How can one tell if it is a dream or a genuine visitation? A visitation is unmistakable in that the spirit of the deceased appears rather suddenly and is generally more vivid, as opposed to an ordinary dream. In terms of my own visitations, the departed loved ones simply stood at the foot of my bed smiling at me, a look of contentment in their eyes. Even more interesting are the spirits of the deceased who choose to make contact with their loved ones face to face.

At the age of nine while visiting relatives in Philadelphia with my paternal grandparents, I woke in the middle of the night to see my maternal great grandfather, "grand-pere" standing at the foot of my bed looking down at me. I loved him dearly and was so happy that he too had made the trip to Philadelphia to join us, although I thought it a bit strange since the two sides of the family never mingled socially. With a smile on my face I fell back into a deep sleep knowing I'd have lots of time the next day to spend with my dear grand-pere. The following morning I jumped out of bed to run into the kitchen where the family gathered, searching for him but he was nowhere to be seen.

"Where's grand-pere?" I asked. Puzzled, the family just looked at me. Again I enquired as to where my grand-pere was and they assured me he was back in Toronto. When I told them I'd seen him the night before in my room they smiled condescendingly and tried to assure me it was just a dream. A few hours later we received the call from Toronto informing us that my dear grand-pere had died the previous evening.

Even more interesting was the experience of my dear grandmother, "Mommie." Widowed at a very young age and living Brooklyn, New York, she had three small children. Her distress increased when, a few days later, she received the news that her father had died in Philadelphia where she'd been born and raised. Alone now, and penniless, she prayed for guidance and within one week of her father's demise she woke in the middle of the night to find him standing at the foot of her bed. He proceeded to give her the name and address of a street in Brooklyn where there would be a job waiting for her. The following day she located the house, and sure enough, there was a sign on the front lawn appealing for a secretary. She applied and was hired on the spot.

There are a myriad of reasons why a departed loved one should wish to make contact with the living; for example, following the demise of my dear brother a few years ago at his home in Utah, I received a call from one of his friends. He and a few of my brother's fishing buddies were planning their annual fishing trip to Muskoka, Ontario, an event like no other according to my brother. His friends expressed their desire to drop by my home on their way up north to present me with some photographs they had of my brother; they were to arrive about 11:30 the following day.

I immediately began straightening up the dining room in preparation for their visit, all the while talking to my brother and expressing my admiration for his ability to boast such fine friends. As I was polishing the dining room table, the sideboard under the window of the room began shaking, so much so that the doors flew open. I knew it was my brother...after all, he'd promised to keep in touch and I know he was delighted that his friends were coming over. When my husband came home that evening I had him check the area around the sideboard for any evidence of problems that might have caused the shaking, but as I expected there were none.

I'd like to add that when my brother informed me of his impending death, I said, "Oh Tommy, I wish there was something I could do," to which he replied,

"It's okay, Judy. Actually, I'm looking forward to the experience."

## THE SAINT THROUGH THE GARDEN GATE

### (A Miracle of Faith)

John Panopoulos was witness to a wonderful miracle of faith granted by his beloved mother. He shares his story with us:

That Easter, while in Church, my mother, Pandora, had a sudden cold sweat come over her and felt uneasy, even when she arrived home. About a month later my mother started to have lower back pain and thought perhaps she had pulled it somehow. As the pain persisted over several weeks we persuaded her to go to the doctor for a checkup. The doctor had prescribed painkillers and muscle relaxant drugs, but the pain persisted. I recall saying to mother as she sat outside in the garden warming her back in the spring sun, "Mom, you must go to the hospital for a proper checkup." Because of mother's reluctance I used the worst-case scenario to try and convince her. "Who knows, it could be cancer," I said.

Immediate tests showed that her blood level was too low, so she was kept in hospital for further analysis. Several days later the doctors revealed that my mother was diagnosed with colon cancer. Surgery was performed shortly after, but by late summer her health had deteriorated and the doctors said that there was no hope for my mother to live for more than a few weeks. Morphine doses were administered for the pain and were increased daily due to the increasing pain. It got to a point that my mother was so drugged she wasn't talking clearly anymore and she slept most of the time.

The doctors could do no more and my family couldn't just sit and watch my mother wither away, waiting for her to die. We were prepared to do almost anything for a remote chance of her recovery. My father, uncle and I went to an herbalist who was known to have helped cure people of many ailments including cancer. Any chance to save my mother was worth no chance at all.

We arranged for mother to stay at the house of my uncle Jim and my aunt Donna, who is my mother's younger sister. My father would also stay there to nurse my mother with a carefully prepared diet and herbs. The morphine was stopped, and within days, she didn't have the intolerable pain and she was once again alert. Her health also seemed to improve over several weeks. As with many Greeks, my aunt Donna has a very strong belief in the Greek Orthodox Church. She would pray for a miracle that Pandora would be saved. Before prayer, a candle would be lit and placed in front of icons of saints known to have cured people. She prayed to the shrines on the Greek Islands of Saint Panaghia of Tinos and Saint Raphael of Metileaneh.

In mid-October my father called home and told us: "Come quickly for your mother had a vision of Saint Raphael of Metileaneh come to her and she believes that she is cured."

When we arrived, there was much joy and tears of happiness. I could hear my mother singing out loud with joy in the bedroom down the hall. I had not seen mother with such brightness in her face and so full of energy since before her illness. My aunt Donna was on the telephone describing the miracle to relations.

My mother described the event to us this way:

"As everyone was asleep at night I awoke facing a beautiful garden; next to the bed was a garden gate where the room wall would normally be. The other side of the garden gate was a path that led through the garden to a tall man in a robe who walked toward me. He was tall, dark haired with large, tranquil, dark eyes. When he reached the gate he spoke in Greek with a clear, soft voice and asked,

'Why are you laying there, my dear Pandora?'

'I'm ill,' I replied.

'You'll be better soon and I will take care of you,' he answered. 'Get up out of bed,' he asked.

'I can't walk,' I said.

'Yes, you can do it,' he again assured me."

Mother got up out of bed by herself and began to walk toward the hall door. My father, Zises, who was sleeping in a bed next to my mother's awoke after having heard someone talking. He was shocked to see my mother walking since she hadn't walked unaided for many months.

"Pandora, what's happening? Where are you going?" he asked.

"Oh I'm fine now, I'm just going to the washroom," she replied.

Mother's appetite and spirits were high after that evening. Over a week later, to the surprise of all, she died peacefully in her sleep one night. I recall the last evening when my mother asked that I just sit next to her so that she could just look at me before falling asleep. When she fell asleep her breathing had become deeper and fainter while her body seemed to get colder, so I rubbed her feet to warm them before I left for the night.

So what happened to the miracle my family and I thought had occurred? Could it be that when my mother's apparition first occurred, it might have been a preparation for her departure from this life?

My mother loved the family so much that she didn't want to die and leave us, so a powerful apparition occurred to persuade my mother to leave her ill body. My mother loved flowers and gardens; she also was religious and believed in saints. I'm convinced that each person leaves this world to the next based upon his or her personal beliefs, which allow a smoother transition for the spirit from one world into another.

My mother's departure from this life would have been another visit from Saint Raphael of Metileaneh; approaching her at the garden gate once more, this time opening it, he would ask my mother to stand up and walk with him along the path among the beautiful gardens. When my mother stood up this time, it was on the garden side of the bed; it was her spirit that stood up, leaving her body behind, and as the garden gate closed, Pandora accepted where she was going.

Lupe Velez was born as Maria Guadalupe Villalobos Velez on July 18, 1908 in Mexico. The daughter of a prostitute, Lupe was sent to Texas at the age of thirteen to live in a convent. Though she dreamed of becoming a champion skater, it was not to be, and she returned to Mexico to work in a department store for $4.00 a week in order to assist her family with their finances. In 1924 she started her career on the Mexican stage. The public was taken with her talent and natural beauty and by 1927 she had moved to Hollywood and was discovered by Hal Roach. He cast her in a comedy with Stan Laurel and Oliver Hardy. She also appeared in three comedies in 1934: *Strictly Dynamite, Palooka* and *Laughing Boy*. So popular was she that a whole series of *Mexican Spitfire* films were written around her.

Eventually, she married one of her lovers, Johnny Weissmuller, but theirs was a union filled with many battles and they divorced after five years. She proceeded to live up to her name and reputation. There was a failed romance with Gary Cooper, who never wanted to wed her, and by 1943 her career was flailing. On December 13, 1944 when her romance with Harold Raymond failed, Lupe, pregnant with Raymond's child, committed suicide with an overdose. She was thirty-six years of age.

In the late 1960's, Jody and her husband, Gabriel, (a musician turned producer) purchased the magnificent Spanish house situated in Los Angeles—the house that had been built by Lupe Velez. Velez had arranged for artisans and craftsmen from Mexico to decorate the house according to her personal taste. The house was situated in Laurel Canyon and the San Fernando Valley, and was built at the time when many actors had weekend retreats in the area. Jody and her husband bought the house from an opera singer who had gone through some hard times. She was the owner of ten cats, and as a result, the house had to be fumigated before they could move in.

According to Jody:

The enormous living room had 18-foot ceiling beams complete with Mexican carvings and paintings; there were French windows to the floor and a courtyard, which was built mostly on terraces because of the hills on Laurel Canyon. It was our first home. Shortly after we moved in, my husband, Gabriel, was recording at the studio. I was doing things around the house and about 2:30 in the morning, I was walking from the kitchen down the hall toward the front of the house where there was a half- circular staircase. From the top of the staircase there was a landing that you could see from the front entry, and from the landing you could walk out through a large balcony through French doors. At the top of the stairs I saw the apparition of a woman dressed in white lace. She didn't do anything. She just stood there. I didn't experience any feelings of negativity although I was startled. I called Gabriel at the studio and asked him to come home. He arrived home around 4:00 a.m. At this time I didn't know the circumstances surrounding Lupe's death; I just knew she had built the house.

Often I would be standing in the kitchen and I had a feeling someone was behind me, but when I turned to look there was no one there. At first I thought perhaps it was Gabriel or perhaps the housekeeper, but when I turned to look there was no one there. Again, I stress that there were no negative feelings whatsoever.

One day I was walking to the little country store with my sheep dog when I met an older gentleman, perhaps in his mid-eighties, who was out working in his garden. He introduced himself to me and it turns out he'd been a cameraman in the film industry and was married at one time to an opera singer who had run off and left him very depressed. He enquired as to how I was enjoying Lupe's house and asked if I had noticed anything strange or unusual about the residence. When I asked him what he meant, he replied, "Oh nothing." Since I felt comfortable with him, I revealed the truth about the strange occurrences that had been happening.

It was then he told me that the previous owners had divulged similar experiences to him. "What do you know about Lupe?" he asked. I told him that I knew she had a shower built into the top of the garage to accommodate the actor Gary Cooper who, although he was one of her lovers, was not allowed to live in the house. I then told him that I knew she had a problem with her weight and constantly had to diet, but disliked it immensely.

The gentleman proceeded to relate the true story surrounding Lupe's untimely death.

According to him, she was a tortured soul who planned to do away with herself, but decided to do it in an extremely elegant manner. She'd apparently ordered an exceptionally elegant peignoir set to be handmade by nuns in Spain, and on the day it arrived, she ordered her live-in cook to prepare all of her favorite foods before dismissing him for the evening. Attiring herself in the splendid peignoir, she proceeded to gorge on the dinner before arranging the bed in such a way as to make herself appear glamorous when her body was discovered. She then swallowed the suicide pills and lay down. But the combination of food and pills spurred an immediate case of diarrhea. Unable to make it to the bathroom, she defecated on the floor, slipped on her defecation, fell, and died when she broke her neck on the toilet.

When I told the gentleman how she would disappear through the French doors onto the terrace, he said that made sense since she would have had to go that way to visit one of her lovers who lived upstairs in the garage which was adjoined to the terrace. He assured me I wasn't crazy.

# LOVELY SPOOKY HAUNTED HOUSE

Carol's experience was fascinating, to say the least. As she tells it to Stephen Wagner who writes an online guide to the paranormal *(Paranormal Phenomena):*

I lived in an old two-story house in a small town called Amonate. This was in 1978. My husband and I rented it from a very old lady. She and her husband had lived there since they were married, but she moved in with her sister, I guess because she was too old to be alone.

I fell in love at once with the house. It was lovely. The lady told me it was very old and that Civil War soldiers had hidden out there during the war. It had a beautiful winding staircase that led up to three bedrooms. I noticed a red stain on the top of the stairs that led down and into the kitchen where a larger stain was. The old gal said her husband had been accidentally shot and the stains were from where he dragged himself down the stairs and made it to the kitchen before dying! Well, that was kinda creepy. I scrubbed and scrubbed, but it would not come off. Downstairs had a living room, kitchen, bath, and a large room I called the ballroom. It had mirrors all around the walls and nothing else except a bar over in a corner. Lots of room for dancing, as I imagined there had been many parties there. We settled in and everything was okay.

The thing I noticed first was that I could never take an afternoon nap upstairs because every time I tried it was as if someone were shaking the bed, so I'd get up. One winter morning, not long after we moved in, I was going to go back to bed after sending my husband off to work. It was still dark outside so I thought I'd lay down for awhile. I decided to leave the light on in the ballroom, which was at the foot of the stairs. I lay down and was getting comfy when I started hearing voices. It was as if there were a large gathering, but far away so that the sounds were muffled. I could hear a man's laughter. It really scared me. My first thought was that someone had broken in to rob me. I grabbed my husband's shotgun and started for the stairs. The hair stood up on my neck as I reached the top of the stairs, for there were no lights on now in the ballroom. The house was very dark. I slowly crept down to the foot of the stairs, now hearing only my heart beating. I quickly flipped the lights back on and there was nothing; not one thing out of place.

Each day around 1:30 p.m., as I would sit down to watch soaps, I could hear footsteps running up the stairs. It happened every day at the same time. This is strange, too. The living room had a large walk-in closet. On the outside of the closet there were half a dozen bolt locks. I wondered why. On the door that led to the living room were several bolt locks also. The fireplace in there had been completely covered over with wallpaper. I took it off, naturally. One day I was cleaning the hearth when I heard dogs—many dogs—as if it were a fox hunt or something. The thing is, the sounds were coming from the fireplace. I ran outside thinking maybe there were dogs barking and the sounds were coming down the chimney, but there were no dogs anywhere and all was quiet. When I returned to the fireplace and bent down, I could still hear the dogs, but they seemed to be getting farther away until the sounds faded away completely.

But the scariest thing of all happened early one morning. As before, my husband went off to work and I went back to bed. It was getting daylight—just so I could see everything, but still not yet daylight. There began this pounding sound as if someone were beating the door down wanting to be let in. I was very scared again, thinking as usual that somebody was trying to break in. So I started downstairs again, shotgun in hand. Only when I got downstairs, the sound was not coming from the front door, but from somewhere in the living room! The pounding was constant, non-stop. I peeked into the room and realized the pounding was in fact coming from inside the closet! It was as if someone were pounding with their fists trying to get out. I yelled, "What do you want?" But the pounding continued. I stood frozen in my tracks for what seemed at least five more minutes and then suddenly, it stopped. It took another five minutes or more to get up the nerve to open the closet door. I was half expecting to see something jump out and grab me, but when I swung open the door, nothing!

I can't explain to you how creepy this was. I wonder to this day if some had been locked in that closet and maybe died there. Why all those locks? We moved after that incident. My husband also felt bad vibes there. Although I loved the house, I just think some really bad things happened there. There were more strange things, but the story is too long to tell. But it is all true.

Upon moving into her new home in Bond Head, Ontario, Mrs. Balsam was taken aback when she walked into the kitchen and saw an Indian in full regalia standing there. Nor was she the only one who viewed the native that occupied the home. The sight of the regal native often bewildered a number of visitors to the home. Since ghosts haunt places and not people, there is a logical explanation in that Bond Head is located on what was once Ojibwa territory. In describing the ghost's attire, Mrs. Balsam mentioned that he wore a feathered headdress, a headdress common to the Ojibwa. It is likely the home had been constructed in the area of an ancient Ojibwa gravesite.

Years later, while caring for her forty-two-year-old son, Jamie, who was gravely ill and was residing with her, Mrs. Balsam strode down the hall toward her son's room in the middle of the night to check on him. Tripping over his body as he lay on the floor in the dark, she was relieved to see that he was still alive. Bending down to assist him, she tearfully pleaded with him not to die. He told her not to worry, saying, "It's okay, Mom." Moments later, he died in her arms.

Returning to the home following her son's funeral, both Mrs. Balsam and her sister were stunned to see Jamie standing in the kitchen looking out the window. Relatives who visited the home saw Jamie's spirit as well. On one occasion, while cooking what used to be her son's favorite meal, Mrs. Balsam heard his voice, loud and clear: "Oh Mom, that smells so good! Taken aback, she turned to see Jamie's spirit standing behind her.

The day I met Mrs. Balsam, she and her sister were holding a garage sale in preparation for her move to another location. As we were chatting, a woman asked if she might use the washroom. Giving her directions to the facilities, Mrs. Balsam and I continued our conversation. A few moments later the woman who had asked to use the washroom walked over to us and enquired: "Who is that nice young man standing in the dining room?" There was no one in the house at the time!

Concerned about moving to another location and deserting her son's spirit, Mrs. Balsam requested my assistance; hence, I communicated with Jamie's spirit, assuring him that he would see his mother again, and following the necessary prayers, it appears that he is finally at rest.

A few days following the burial of her husband, Mrs. Norris and her three companions were in the kitchen at her home. Suddenly, the old grandfather clock in the hall stuck twelve. Since the clock hadn't worked in years, Mrs. Norris was obviously perplexed. Going into the hall to see what was happening, she noted that the clock face showed 2:20 and the pendulum was slowly swinging. About three months later while driving her car, she was startled to hear the voice of her deceased husband criticizing her driving and telling her not to drive so fast! Glancing over to the passenger's seat, she saw him sitting there.

A few years later Mrs. Norris was mourning the loss of her dear friend, Neil, who had died suddenly. It wasn't long before some of her friends informed her that they'd seen Neil's spirit. Another friend, Roger, told her he had spoken with Neil's spirit. With a beaming smile, Neil had asked him: "Is there anyone you know who is pregnant? I think I'll try again."

Her friend Sarah then saw Neil walking in a wonderful place and said, "Where are you?"

"Where do you think I am?" Neil responded.

"Is Jesus with you?" asked Sarah.

"Do you think I'd be here if he wasn't?" answered Neil.

Her friend, Jennie, was the most comprehending. Upon visiting Mrs. Norris for lunch one day, Jennie insisted, that they go see where Neil had died before they had lunch. According to Mrs. Norris, "insisted" is a very poor word; she was almost frantic in her doggedness.

As she led the way, Jennie commented: "He came here. No-o-o not that way, over here—yes, right here." She was standing on the exact spot where the car he had died in had been parked. Looking up she said: "Yes, those trees were right there, and over here was something black, but it's not here."

"Oh, yes," replied Mrs. Norris, "A black horse trailer was parked there."

"That's it," said Jennie, and turning back she looked up at her friend and said, "Two angels came down for him and I thought to myself, *Why does he get two angels when other people only get one?*"

Some time later, Mrs. Norris gave Jennie a card that depicted a beautiful blue sunset that their friend Roger had painted. Jennie turned absolutely white saying, "That's it! That's exactly what I saw when the angels came for Neil."

According to Mrs. Norris: "The only thing that came to me was a startling realization that the spot where he died had the aura of a holy place. My son was skeptical, but when I insisted he come and see for himself, he could feel it too." On the day of Neil's memorial, almost everyone went up to the spot and everyone could feel a presence.

I could feel it for well over a month until it gradually faded away. The weather grew cooler until one cool day, Mrs. Norris, at a loss for words, stood at her kitchen window and watched in amazement as a branch from one of her rosebushes outside the window sketched the name of her dear, departed friend Neil onto the frosty glass.

Susan lives in Schomberg, Ontario, and when a very close friend of hers lost his wife, she was concerned for his health, as his depression appeared to be increasing over time. In an attempt to assuage his mourning, she tried to spend as much time as possible with him, but noticed he was definitely going downhill psychologically. Susan attributed his downhill slide to the fact that he had absolutely no faith in the possibility of an afterlife.

About six weeks following the death of his wife, her spirit, along with the spirit of Susan's grandmother (who appeared to her often), visited Susan. Obviously concerned about her husband's mental state, the spirit asked Susan to please tell him she would be waiting for him when it was his turn to pass over. Susan noticed she was attired in flowered pajamas, an observation that would eventually shed more light on the situation. The spirit also mentioned that she used to get very upset when her husband would "dog-ear" the pages of books as opposed to using a bookmark. This was the spirit's way of leaving a clue as to her reality, a common procedure most spirits employ to define their reality.

When Susan mentioned the "page bending" to her friend he admitted it and began to cry. He also, during the course of their conversation, mentioned that his wife was wearing flowered pajamas when she died. As well, Susan noticed that whenever she had a conversation with her friend's deceased wife, she was in a cottage in an area she perceived to be northern Ontario. When she mentioned this to her friend, he described his cottage in Muskoka, Ontario, and lo and behold, it was the same cottage, a revelation that led Susan's friend on the road to a belief in the afterlife.

On another occasion, a male spirit appeared to Susan and as she describes it, "he was standing there holding an old-fashioned glass with double scotch on the rocks!" The spirit was holding the particular type of glass to identify himself to Susan and the party to whom he wished to contact. It seems that he, too, had a message to pass on to a loved one through Susan. However, in the meantime, Susan was having a difficult time sleeping as she began to experience nightmares and appeared to be surrounded by negative spirits. She would find the hair on the back of her neck standing up with fear as cold gusts of wind blew in her direction at any time of the night or day. She had numerous candles throughout her home, but was extremely careful and made sure they were extinguished at night before she retired. She had a friend stay with her on one occasion, and when he arose one morning he was shocked to come downstairs and find a few of the candles had been lit! Seeking advice from a psychic, Susan was advised to burn sage, a spiritual ritual that terminated the unpleasant visits.

According to the *Toronto Ghosts & Hauntings Research Society*, the old Don Jail in Toronto is home to the tormented spirit of a prisoner who committed suicide there. "The Don" was the main holding area in Toronto for men and women as well as the ghost of a female prisoner with long blonde hair who hung herself in one of the small cells. Her spirit floats around the main rotunda of the building and is reported to be extremely agitated. In Columbo's book, *Haunted Toronto,* he reports that journalist, Tracy Tyler, believes the spirit remains this way because she feels "trapped in time.

In November of 2005, a Corrections Officer who was employed at the infamous house of detention experienced an event that was extremely weird. For those not acquainted with the interior of the Don Jail (actually the newer section which was constructed in the late 1950s was originally named the Toronto Jail even though it is physically attached to the older 1863 building) the detention areas are set up in the following manner There are many units that are identical to the following layout. There are two rows of approximately ten cells back to back with each row facing out into a barred "day area" where inmates are allowed to take limited exercise.

Resembling a box within a box, the cells are barred and the day area is also barred. The corrections officer sits in a control booth just outside that area where they can observe the inmates as well as lock and unlock the two doors which are the only way in and out. Like an air lock on a submarine, these doors cannot be opened at the same time. The outer door is opened and then secured before the inner door is opened and access to the day area is allowed.

There is also an area where the guards circle the prisoners' area allowing them to safely view both the day area and the cells where the inmates are locked in at night. These "rounds" take place every twenty minutes for the dual purpose of verifying the prisoners' presence as well as their well-being. In the middle of the day area and securely chained to the ceiling is a large, heavy punching bag. The chain makes an unmistakably loud rattling sound when the bag is being pummeled.

It was approximately 2:00 in the morning when, during one of the required rounds, an inmate called out to the guard that he had been awakened by someone "hitting the bag." Even though the light in the area is dimmed during the night hours it remains bright enough for the guard to see clearly into the cells. When the prisoner made his nocturnal complaint the guard had a clear view of the prisoner and the punching bag. The guard had not heard the obvious and familiar sound of the bag being used and he quickly walked back to the beginning of the circle and began head count. If the bag had been hit it meant that an inmate was able to get out of his supposedly locked cell and into the day area. As everyone was accounted for, the inmate was told to go back to sleep.

Twenty minutes later, during the next set of rounds, the inmate complained again. The guard looked directly at the silent, stationary punching bag and then repeated the strong suggestion that the inmate should go back to sleep. The guard then went on break after warning the relief officer of the recent events. The guard was surprised to be called back early from break by the relief officer who reported that two inmates were now complaining of being awakened by someone hitting the bag in the enclosed area. The relief officer had decided a check of the cell doors inside the day area was required. This procedure meant the two double security doors to the day area be unlocked from the control booth by a second guard. The check was quickly made and all the cell doors were found to be secure with all inmates present and accounted for.

This should have been the end of it, except that on one of the next sets of rounds—this time with two other officers present—the heavy, previously stationary punching bag was swinging back and forth. There was no sound from the chain and there was no possible way an inmate, even with a long broom handle, could have stretched out through the cell bars and even reached the bag let alone have pushed it hard enough to make it swing at the rate it was observed.

## SUNNYSIDE BEACH

It was a crisp fall day in 1944 when the witness decided to meet her then boyfriend on the boardwalk at Sunnyside Beach in Toronto. During the war years it was a popular place for young couples, much as it is today. It was nearing twilight when the witness and her beau noticed a strange young woman approaching them from the shadows of the Canoe Club. What struck them as odd was the fact she was dressed in a long black dress to her ankles (inappropriate for a young lady in that era) with no coat despite the chilliness of the air. As well, her hair was rather longish (past her shoulders) which was uncommon, as most women and girls of the day were cropping their hair in much shorter styles. The odd young lady appeared as if out of nowhere, and as she came closer they noted how pale she was. She lifted the front of her dress and began to climb the grassy hill towards the boardwalk.

The couple began to follow the girl and were astonished as she entered the street that was busy with traffic. To their horror she crossed the road completely ignoring the cars as if they did not exist. Expecting to hear the sounds of slamming brakes and car horns they were equally mystified when this did not occur. As soon as it was safe to cross they ran across the street hoping to catch sight of the mysterious young woman who, seemingly, had just defied certain injury or death. However, she had vanished. In those days, on the far end of the road there were train tracks and a lengthy bridge to cover before coming anywhere near a house or another structure.

The couple were convinced that, even had she been running at top speed, they would have caught sight of her. The strangeness of the event and the lady's apparent sudden disappearance led them to believe that they had both just witnessed a ghost. Unnerved, they began meeting elsewhere…and they did not see this "apparition" again. (*Toronto Ghosts & Hauntings Research Society.*)

Irene Cooper had just moved from Newfoundland to New Brunswick and was living in a flat above a store with her two sisters and children. There were empty rooms upstairs from her apartment, which she later learned had been the scene of a gruesome murder. She awoke one night to the sound of a cat meowing and hissing only to find that the sounds were emanating from the spirit of a woman with very long claws and a black hood hovering right above her.

On another occasion, Irene and her sisters saw the spirit of a woman walking through their flat only to disappear through the wall, and not long after that, another woman with copious amounts of blood dripping from her was silently strolling down the hall.

Unable to go to work one day as she was feeling ill, Irene's sister spent the day at home in her room, but found it impossible to rest because of the sound of paper rattling all day. That evening she approached Irene and asked, "Why would you let the kids make that noise all day when you knew I was feeling ill"?

Irene just looked at her and responded, "The kids were at school all day, there was no one here but yourself."

## THE FORMER LAKESHORE PSYCHIATRIC HOSPITAL

Another building well-known for its ghostly activity is located just a few blocks from my childhood home in what used to be Mimico, Ontario, but is now called Etobicoke. The old Lakeshore Psychiatric Hospital, originally known as the Mimico Hospital for the Insane, or Mimico Asylum, is infamous for its numerous hauntings reported by construction workers, utility workers, former visitors, and so on.

Built during the late 1880's, the high stone walls of the institution proved to be a challenge to my brother and me as we attempted numerous times to scale the walls as youngsters. Although we were too young to understand the concept of an asylum, we knew there was something weird and uncanny occurring within the walls of the large building behind the stone stockade. The mournful sounds of howling and weeping were constantly reaching our ears, leading us to wonder what was happening inside the mysterious building.

Although the very word "asylum" gives one the impression that the building and grounds were ugly and unkempt, nothing could be further from the truth. Both building and grounds were exquisitely assembled, fitting right in with the neighbouring mansions in the area. Postcards from the early twentieth century testify to the superb village-like complex surrounded by colorful flowerbeds and an array of picturesque trees. Although the site of the building has been taken over by Humber College, the layouts of the original structures remain the same.

It appears that shortly after the renovation of three of the old buildings, a couple of students, having decided to explore the tunnels connecting the buildings, heard a distinct whistling sound. Every time they turned around to investigate, the sound ceased, and as they reached the stairs to go up, they heard it again, followed by a cold gust of wind.

One of the construction workers assigned to the same tunnels was walking through the hallway only to spot a woman in a nurse's uniform walking in front of him. He thought this was strange as it was very late and there was no one else working at the time. Calling out to her, he watched as she went around a corner and disappeared. Curious, he followed her, only to find her standing at the far end of the hallway with her back to him. It was physically impossible for her to have moved that far in the short time he had lost sight of her. He approached her cautiously and called out again. He watched as she slowly turned around to face him. Terrified, the hapless workman observed that she had no face; only a flat blank area where her face should have been. He turned and ran from the apparition, refusing to return to work in the tunnels again.

It is interesting to note that the Afritans of the Shari River in Central America would blindfold a corpse before burying it to prevent it from returning to haunt the survivors.

## GHOST CALLS

Telephone calls from the dead? Not only do they transpire, they occur with a frequency that surpasses most other psychic experiences.

Researchers have determined that the phenomenon usually occur within the first twenty-four hours of death, although there have been cases in which the calls were received as long as two years after. Generally, they occur when the recipient of the call is in a relaxed, almost sleep-like state. In such calls, the telephone usually rings normally, but may sound flat and abnormal. The call can last anywhere from one to five minutes. More often than not the calls are directed to a relative of the deceased and often occur on special days such as anniversaries, Mother's Day or birthdays. The phone connection is generally unusually static and the voice of the deceased fades quickly, and more often than not, dissipates altogether.

There have also been cases where the call has been placed long distance and connected by the operator. Upon checking with the phone company there is no evidence of such a call being made. Though extremely rare, there have been cases where the phantom answers the phone.

In one case, the recipient of the call was fast asleep. It was a Sunday morning and the ringing of the phone woke him. It was his grandmother enquiring as to his health as he had been hospitalized for a few weeks previous to the call. She also asked if he had been informed of the death of a relative who had lived in another state, to which he answered, no. Telling him how much she loved him, the grandmother ended the call leaving the man in question speechless. You see, she called on his birthday, which happened to be the sixth anniversary of her death.

## FEAR OF GHOSTS

The term "phasmophobia" means *fear of ghosts*. There are those who fear them so much they would do anything to deny their very existence. To these individuals I feel compelled to stress that they will never harm you. When it comes to children, it is vitally important that you never laugh or tease them as ghosts are very definitely attracted to children and the child's fears are more than likely founded. Never, ever laugh at the child. Instead, allow them to move to another room to let them sleep and allow them to keep the light on all night if they wish. Make sure they know you are going to be checking on them at various intervals during the night, and above all, believe what they say, otherwise the experience could leave the child psychologically scarred. Above all, do not—in any way shape or form, challenge a ghost. Believe me…I know from whence I speak!

So ancient is the fear of ghosts that various methods have been devised to ensure they are kept at bay. Among them are:

1. Always have available certain metals such as silver, as well as salt.

2. To prevent a ghost from "rising from the grave," place an iron rod on the grave.

3. To rid your home of ghosts, place an iron horseshoe above the door.

4. When someone passes away in a home, all doors, windows and cupboards should be unlocked to allow the ghost free passage from the house and the body must be carried from the home feet first to ensure it won't return.

5. And last, but far from least, never speak poorly of the dead.

## HOUSE CLEARINGS

There are those who opt to appoint someone to come into their homes to "clear" it from such disturbances. There are para-researchers (such as myself), as well as ministers and priests, who are equipped to do a "house clearing." Christianity has continued to acknowledge the likelihood of ghosts and spirits and the service of exorcism is still employed for driving out those spirits that are deemed harmful. Catholics, in particular, appear to have a great deal of information on the subject.

# GHOST COFFINS

"Ghost coffins" is a term used to describe heavy, lead coffins that have been sealed inside crypts and yet are able to move themselves from place to place. It would be literally impossible for just one person to move the coffin and yet they are often found in disarray as if a violent force had thrown them about. Though restored to their natural location they are again found in disorder when the vaults are reopened. Granted, it has been determined in a couple of cases that the movement was caused by the flooding of the crypts, but aside from that no other logical explanation has been established, other than the fact that these disturbances often occur in a vault where one of the buried had committed suicide. Others speculate that the ghosts of the dead disturb the coffins, expressing their dislike of where they have been buried. Still others think that the deceased, who don't want to be in the same vault as another particular person, may cause it.

All extra-physical beings are individuals of a heightened level of awareness, whose intentions for us are positive, in an evolutionary manner. Unfortunately, the names given them such as helpers, spirit guides, guardian angels, protectors or masters, have religious or mystical associations, yet there is nothing mystical about them. Like us, they are individuals who are expressing a high level of maturity and lucidity during their period between lives, and like us, are still evolving and will have future lives. They specialize in helping others in need and their good deeds are exemplified by their discretion and respect for the free will of all individuals.

# BODY DOUBLES

Another strange paranormal occurrence is that of the appearance of an individual in advance of his or her arrival, even to the point of wearing the same clothes. Commonly known as a "wraith" or "arrival ghost," the legendary Mark Twain reported experiencing such an incident. Having met a woman he knew at a reception, he then met with her at dinner later on. However, the real woman was held up on a train that was running late and arrived late to the reception.

Is it possible for an individual to be in two places at the same time? There are numerous accounts throughout history that would swear it's true. These people claim either to have encountered apparitions of themselves (doppelgangers) or found themselves in two separate locations at the same time. The term "doppelganger" is German for *double walker*—a replica of oneself that is believed to accompany every living individual. As a rule, the phantom self can only be seen by the owner and in many cases has proven to be a harbinger of death. Stranger still, reports of friends and family seeing the double have also been recorded throughout time—an experience that obviously leaves the viewers extremely confused since the double is indistinguishable from the real person and is able to converse and interact with others.

Julie Von Guldenstubbe, the second daughter of Baron Von Guldenstubbe, told American author, Dale Owen, this story. At the age of thirteen, Julie was a student at Pensionat Von Neuwelcke, an exclusive girl's school near Wolmar, now Latvia. One of Julie's teachers, Emilie Sagee, a thirty-two-year-old French woman was looked up to by the school's administration until she began to become the target of rumor and weird accounts. According to thirteen of her students, Sagee had a double that would simultaneously appear and disappear in full view of her classes.

While writing on the blackboard one day, her exact double suddenly appeared beside her, mimicking precisely every movement as she wrote on the board; however, the doppelganger (or double) held no chalk. While having dinner one evening, Sagee's double appeared standing behind her and mimicked every movement of her eating although it had no utensils.

The doppelganger, however, didn't always copy Sagee's movements. On more than one occasion, Sagee was spotted in one area of the school when everyone knew full well she was in another. One summer day in 1846, forty-two students were seated at long tables in the school hall working on their sewing and embroidery lessons. They were able to see Sagee gathering flowers outside in the garden. Their sewing teacher had an appointment with the headmistress and had no sooner left the hall when Sagee's doppelganger sat in the chair. Looking outside, the students were still able to see Sagee in the garden, but according to her movements she appeared to be extremely tired. The doppelganger sat motionless in the chair. Finally, a couple of the girls approached the double and attempted to touch it, but were unable to as their was some sort of blockage in the air. One of the girls actually stepped between the desk and the teacher's chair, passing right through the apparition that remained motionless before slowly dissipating. Although Sagee never laid eyes on the doppelganger herself, it was established that every time it appeared, she felt exhausted, even to the point where her physical color paled.

There have been numerous cases of doppelgangers appearing to famous individuals, a few of which are listed below.

**Guy de Maupassant:** French novelist and short story writer. Near the end of his life he claimed to have constantly seen his doppelganger and on one occasion, his double entered his room, sat opposite him and began to dictate what de Maupassant was currently writing, an experience the author wrote about in his short story, "Lui."

**John Donne:** The 16th century English poet whose work often touched on the metaphysical, was visited by a double when he was in Paris. However, the double wasn't his; it was that of his wife! The doppelganger was holding a newborn infant, and although Donne's wife was pregnant at the time, the apparition was a portent of great sadness since his wife had given birth to a stillborn baby girl at the same time the double appeared.

**Percy Byshe Shelley:** Considered one of the greatest poets of all time, he encountered his double while in Italy. Oddly enough, the doppelganger was pointing toward the Mediterranean Sea. Another sad portent, as shortly before his thirtieth birthday in 1822, Shelley drowned in the Mediterranean Sea as a result of a sailing accident.

**Queen Elizabeth 1 of England:** Her Majesty was shocked to see her double laid out on her bed. She died shortly after.

## GHOST CURSES

James Dean, the famous movie star of the 1950's, lived his life in the fast lane, much like the roles he portrayed on screen. He purchased a silver gray 1955 Porsche Spyder that he'd planned on racing at Salinas. Although Dean was thrilled with his new car, for some reason, a number of his friends weren't. Actor Alec Guiness advised him to get rid of the car and George Barris stated that the car appeared to give off "a weird feeling of impending doom."

During a trip out of Los Angeles, Rolf Wuetherich rode with Dean while behind them, following in a Ford station wagon was Stan Roth and Bill Hickman. When they reached the open highway Dean sped up until finally a highway trooper pulled over the Porshe and presented Dean with a ticket. Continuing their trip, Dean and Wuetherich began the ascent of the Diablo Range Mountains when suddenly Dean smashed head on into another car driven by Donald Turnupseed. Dean was killed instantly. Although Wuetherich did survive, he did suffer extensive injuries. The Porsche was very badly damaged.

The car was later sold to Barris who planned to use the parts for spares, but when the car was being unloaded at the garage it fell, breaking the leg of one of the mechanics. Two doctors then purchased the engine and drive train and placed them in their own racecars. On October 2nd, 1956, they raced the cars for the first time. One was killed in an accident and the other, seriously injured in an accident. Two of the tires from Dean's car were then sold to a young man who reported later that both tires had blown at exactly the same time very nearly causing a serious accident.

Fans seeking memorabilia then attempted to steal parts from Dean's car, suffering injuries in the process. Deciding to display Dean's car as part of a safety exhibit, The California Highway Patrol had the car placed with other cars in a garage used as part of the exhibit. Without any explanation, the garage burned down, destroying all the vehicles inside except Dean's car.

A short time later, while on display at a Sacramento High School, the car fell from its pedestal, breaking the hip of a student. After that, the car was being shipped to Salinas when it fell off the flat bed truck and killing the driver. Two years later it fell off another truck causing an accident. Responsible for another accident in 1958, the car was finally on display again in 1959 when, for no apparent reason, it suddenly collapsed into eleven pieces.

Finally, in 1960, the car was crated and sent to Los Angeles, but mysteriously it never arrived; it simply disappeared.

## INCUBUS

An incubus is a spirit who indulges in sexual intercourse with living females. The concept might have derived from the idea of the commerce of gods with women, a prevalent train of thought in those days. For mediaeval and modern occurrences we refer to the writings where they are found; the very names of the writers will more than avouch for their credibility. The history of Hector Boece contains about four significant examples, which obtain confirmation from the pen of Cardan. In one of these he writes...

"in the chamber of a young gentlewoman of excellent beauty,

and the daughter of a nobleman, in a country of Mar, was found at an unseasonable hour 'a foule monstrous thing,' very horrible to behold, for the love of which…the lady had refused sundry wealthy marriages. A priest who was in the company began to repeat St. John's Gospel, and ere he had proceeded far 'suddenly the wicked spirit, making a very sore and terrible roaring noise, flue his waies, taking the roof of the chamber away with him, the hangings and coverings of the bed being also burnt therewith.'"

## SUCCUBUS

A succubus is a demon that takes the shape of a woman. The Rabbi Elias says that it is mentioned in certain writings that Adam was visited during one hundred and thirty years by female demons, and had intercourse with demons, spirits, specters, lemurs and phantoms. Under the reign of Roger, king of Sicily, a young man, bathing by moonlight, with several others, thought he saw someone drowning, and hastened to the rescue. Having drawn from the water, a beautiful woman, he became enamored of her, married her, and had by her, a child. Afterwards, she disappeared mysteriously with her child, which made everyone believe that she was a succubus.

Hector Boece also relates in his history of Scotland that a very handsome young man was pursued by a female demon who would pass through his closed door and offer to marry him. He complained to his Bishop, who advised him to fast, pray and confess himself when the infernal visitor ceased to trouble him.

Delancre says that in Egypt, an honest man was occupied in forging when during the night there appeared to him a demon under the shape of a beautiful woman. He threw a hot iron into the face of the demon, which at once took flight.

# TWO

## Dreams

Hard as it is to believe, by age seventy-five you will have spent twenty-five years sleeping and nearly half that time, twelve and a half years, dreaming. There is no question that Intuition is the language of our dreams. We all dream during the REM states of sleep which occur every ninety minutes or so during the night. Our dreams provide us with information about our health, relationships, and virtually every area of our lives. In other words, our dreams provide us with a wealth of information and it behooves everyone to keep a dream diary by their bed. Every night, just before sleep, ask a dream question such as, "Is this the right relationship for me"? The following morning, jot down the remembered dreams before you get out of bed. Repeat the same question every night and eventually the answer will be revealed to you...generally within a week or so.

Although there are numerous types of dreams, I have listed those dreams that are classified as psychic.

## PRECOGNITIVE DREAMS

It has been scientifically established that that as many as 65 percent of precognitive experiences occur during the sleep state. As well, the precognitive dream provides more complete and accurate information than waking psychic experiences. Since the majority of our dreams are generally quite mundane, it is possible for the dreamer to receive accurate glimpses of the future while sleeping. Some people choose to keep a dream diary and are therefore able to check which of their dreams come true. A very small percentage of individuals have the ability to know which of their dreams are precognitive; however, this is quite rare. There are dreams that seem to anticipate a later unexpected event, which could not reasonably have been inferred from available information at the time of the dream. About 40 percent of reported psychic experiences concern knowing the future in some way.

Premonitions come in the form of dreams, waking thoughts, waking imagery and sleep onset (hypnogogic) imagery; however, the most frequent vehicle is that of the dream. Premonition dreams have been reported throughout all recorded human history. They were recorded on cuneiform-script clay tablets by the ancient Assyrians and Babylonians as well as being accepted in ancient Egyptian, Greek and Roman civilizations. Even in the bible, several significant dreams were recorded, which offered valuable information at times of crisis or warnings of future dangers. One such dream was that of the Pharaoh who dreamed of seven fat and seven thin cattle. Joseph deciphered it as meaning that seven years of plentiful harvest would be followed by seven years of famine. The Pharaoh built up food stocks and saved the country.

It has been recorded, for example, that in September of 1981, a woman named Barbara Garwell dreamt of a group of dignitaries in a stadium in a country in the Middle East. She watched as a group of soldiers scurried up to the rows of dignitaries and sprayed them with automatic gunfire. On the 6th of October 1981, twenty-one days later, President Anwar Sadat of Egypt was assassinated and several others had been killed or injured at an identical event commemorating the 1973 Yom Kippur war with Israel.

The philosophical quandary in terms of premonitions is, of course, that the knowledge of the event precedes the event itself. This is a theoretical impossibility to current conventional science, just as it was thought impossible that the sun didn't rotate around the earth. As mentioned, I've had more than my share of precognitive dreams, and am happy to say they have always been of a pleasing nature. Not so with Mark Twain's precognitive dream, which involved viewing his brother's body enclosed in a coffin. Less than a week later his brother died as a result of a boat explosion.

Following the disastrous fate of the Titanic, there were numerous reports of relieved individuals who had canceled their trip as a result of their precognitive dreams about the sinking. One man, an extremely busy corporate executive, dreamed of the sinking five times yet chose to ignore it. Just prior to his intended trip something came up that prevented him from boarding the ship. One has to wonder how many other individuals experienced the same dream yet chose to just write it off. When the characters in a precognitive dream are individuals other than us, it is wise to deduce that the meaning of the dream is a message to ourselves. Also, a precognitive dream can assist us to prepare for an event that would otherwise be an enormous shock to the conscious mind. For example, several years ago in Kansas City, a bridge collapsed in a large hotel. A number of individuals later reported dreaming of the catastrophe prior to its occurrence. As a result of their dreams, they altered their plans and chose not to attend the event that was occurring at the hotel. They chose to protect themselves from danger, thus, they were able to be of assistance to those involved.

There is no question that precognitive dreams can foretell the future. Unlike our physical mind that is inhibited by the laws of physics and physical limitations, our subconscious mind is able to perceive the probable future by tracking the flow of consciousness forward. The future is probable rather than predestined as we have free will and are able to alter our future by the choices we make. A precognitive dream occurs when the subconscious mind perceives the probable future. Some individuals may experience this as "déjà vu" which means *already seen.* When we have precognitive dreams and then experience the same occurrence we've previously dreamt about, it naturally feels familiar since we've already seen it in our dreams.

Precognitive dreams (sometimes known as "premonition dreams") have been recorded throughout history, carved onto cuneiform-clay tablets by the ancient Assyrians and Babylonians, and were accepted in Roman, Egyptian and Greek civilizations as well. Extensive research into the study of premonitions revealed that the receivers are mainly female and the premonitions, more often than not, concern problematic events that will happen to those closest to them. This was not the case however, when J.L Chaffin (Anon, 1927) appeared to his disinherited son in a dream, giving him clues as to where he could locate a second will. The will was found and recognized by the court, thereby restoring the inheritance to the dreamer.

About 40 percent of psychic dreams inform dreamers of future events and though premonitions come to us during the hypnogogic state (the state just prior to sleep), the most common vehicle is the dream.

## HEALING DREAMS

One of the most fascinating types of dream is the Healing Dream. Take, for example, the personal experience of Wanda E. Burch as she writes in her book, *She Who Dreams:*

At the beginning of 1990, I followed my dreams to Africa. I was in Ghana when I fell asleep on a warm afternoon, lulled in and out of awareness by the syncopated beating of yams in the Asantemanso village dooryards. I dreamed a warning dream, more literal and more terrifying than any of my previous dreams.

My father, who had died the year before of colon cancer, appears and seems to be checking on me. Someone else is also in the dream, a man dressed in a medical coat. He tells me, almost shouting, that I have a malignant lump in my breast and that I must have my breast removed. He is still shouting at me. He tells me that no matter what I hear, that it is not benign. He is now leading me out the door, almost pulling me, telling me we are going to the Mayo Clinic where another doctor is shouting to me that I have a malignancy and that I must act immediately. This dream had followed almost two years of carefully recorded dreams filled with symbols and images of illness that I failed to understand and to act upon. The new dream drove me to consult with physicians as soon as I got home. They detected breast cancer; a variety that was fast-moving, non-massing, and aggressive. My condition required immediate surgery, the removal of my left breast.

Robert Moss, in *Conscious Dreaming*, discusses the dream that finally brings the conscious mind to attention; the dream that finally kicks you awake because you have not remembered, not understood, or not paid appropriate heed to an important dream or series of dreams.

Now that I had learned from my own dream wake-up call, I began to ask other men and women who had experienced serious illness if they recalled a particular dream or intuitive moment that had helped to alert them to their condition or guided their healing. Many of the people I interviewed were women who had suffered breast cancer. Their stories were as varied and individual as the dreamers themselves and ranged from little bears helping with house cleaning to dramatic stories of physical and spiritual loss and rebirth played out in dreaming and in waking.

When we finally feel confident in exploring the elements of dream diagnosis, the next step is to explore the elements of healing in our dreams. Diagnosis is presented not to frighten us, but to allow us to begin a journey of healing. Once the problem is diagnosed and acknowledged, the dreams begin to change, offering the symbols and metaphors each of us can use for recovery and healing. Healing is not always connected with staying alive, and that is sometimes the most difficult lesson to learn; healing is sometimes a preparation for death. Healing dreams give us images unique to our own personal mythology that can be used like a prescription in the healing process.

Galen [of Pergamum] believed one could study a patient's imagery and dream content and learn important diagnostic information that could help the patient learn to heal themselves and bring their bodies and minds back into balance. The Renaissance physician Paracelsus, who attributed his understanding of health and illness to conversations with women, wrote about the power of the imagination as one of the greatest factors in medicine. He noted that the imagination could both produce disease and cure disease. He also believed in the magic of using medical knowledge in conjunction with the power of the spirit working through the soul.

The day I was diagnosed with breast cancer, I came home and walked into my empty house alone, angry, afraid, and confused. I lay down on the sofa and desperately tried to think of what to do first. I closed my eyes, almost, but not quite, drifting to sleep and had a dream in which I held my left breast over a pan of water, turning it over, pointing to the exact location of the cancer, and squeezing the breast like a sponge into the water, dark fluid flowing into the bowl.

That image, pinpointing the location of my cancer, and the image of squeezing the sponge breast until the poisonous liquid flowed into the bowl, became my first healing images. When my surgeon, a man who understood the healing process, told me to go home and do something to begin my healing, I took those images and used them every day and every evening until my biopsy. I used them like a prescription, stating an intention of healing, and imagining the dark fluid being pulled into one place where it could be controlled and eliminated. I began the process of using my dream images to save my life.

Healing can be a creative journey; when it comes in a dream, healing imagery is a special gift. In the midst of my own healing I had a wonderful dream in which I was in an enormous room filled with tools. The tools took on a life of their own and at the end of this dream I joined them in a magnificent ballet of active healing. The ballet was performed in the air in a classroom and the entire dream was so permeated with magic and healing images that I felt, when I woke, that there was no barrier between my mind and my body, that they were indeed working in a magical harmony to effect the healing and balance of both. This dream helped me form intent in my mind.

Scan your dreams for diagnosis and for the symbols and images needed for your healing. You will find there a direct correlation between intent and dreaming images and you will be able to chart a course for healing. In our daily communication with one another, we share language symbols that we each recognize and use for fluid communication. Our dreams give us a different set of symbols that our sleeping self must share with our waking self so that communication with the body can continue beyond the dream.

Once we begin to recognize and understand our own unique set of images in our sleep dreams, then we can begin to translate them in the day and use them to create active healing.

## CHARACTERS IN OUR DREAMS

Dream research conducted by the School of Metaphysics verifies that everyone in a dream is an aspect or quality of the dreamer. For example, a spouse represents the inner subconscious self; an infant or child represents a fresh beginning, new idea or a change in your life. A majority of people (58.5%) reported dreaming of others who are currently in their lives while 25.2% reported dreaming primarily about individuals from their past. You will dream of individuals in your current life when you spend time with them, and when the qualities you perceive in them are duplicated within your own character.

Since every dream we have relates only to us, the presence or absence of certain individuals in our dreams specify the areas that are a part of your awareness. For example, more than one-tenth of respondents (12.2%) reported dreaming of their minister the least often. This would occur because the minister symbolizes one's higher or spiritual self, and a dreamer who has not made spirituality a part of their conscious awareness is not likely to dream often of such a person. When primarily people from your past populate your dreams, much of your thinking and attention is in the past. When you learn to bring your attention into the present, these dreams will change.

## VISITATION DREAMS

It is not uncommon for a recently deceased relative or friend to visit us in a dream. (As aforementioned, this phenomenon has happened to me on a number of occasions.) Research shows that when a deceased person communicates in a dream through telepathy or other nonverbal means, that entity is communicating to the dreamer in the dream state. If the deceased person speaks and their mouth moves, then they represent some aspect of the dreamer. A majority (52.8%) of those surveyed have dreamt of departed relatives or friends. Nearly one-third (30%) believe the dream was a visitation from the deceased and 36.6% said the person spoke to them in the dream, often offering reassurance and comfort.

Some of the impressions described from such dreams are: "comforting"; "a loving experience"; "He spoke to me to comfort me and tell me he was happy—I believed him"; "It felt comforting to have dreamed of my grandfather who had passed away"; "I felt like they were trying to make me at peace with something going on or a past issue"; and "I felt it was their spirit actually speaking to me. It was very positive and loving."

These dreams, as the statistics indicate, are normal and are usually comforting rather than frightening. They can help us resolve some of our questions about death, showing that life exists beyond the physical existence and that we are never truly separated from those we love nor from the love within ourselves.

## REPETITIVE DREAMS

Repetitive dreams and nightmares have a great deal in common. They both occur as a result of the subconscious mind attempting to relay an important message to the dreamer. If the same dream persists for a period of months or even years, it is a sure sign there are issues in your life that must be resolved.

## NIGHTMARES

The majority of individuals I've interviewed reported suffering from nightmares. Quite often, a nightmare is merely a result of the subconscious mind attempting to relay a message to the dreamer that is being ignored; in other words, the nightmare is literally "screaming" to get your attention by shocking you into recalling the dream. By interpreting your dream messages (to the best of your ability) you are better able to understand exactly what it is your subconscious is attempting to convey to you, and as a result, your nightmare will cease. In other words, the more we nurture our self-awareness, the fewer nightmares we will experience as our conscious awareness is now united with the truth within our subconscious mind.

## COMMON NIGHTMARES AND THEIR MEANINGS

1.  Being chased by an unknown person: This is the most common type of nightmare, an indication to the dreamer that there is a part of you that you are unwilling to face. Only when you have learned to face yourself, will these nightmares cease.

2.  Being trapped or paralyzed: This type of dream indicates that the dreamer (in his or her waking state) feels that they are limited as to their choices in life. However, it is simply the dreamer's lack of imagination that is the real culprit since, chances are, their thinking is negative and they are filled with self-doubt and/or hesitation. It is imperative that these individuals learn to interact with others, thereby stimulating his or her imagination and learning to make choices in life. Even more important, they must learn to act on the choices they have made.

## REMEMBERING YOUR DREAMS

Almost half of those surveyed recall dreaming more than four nights a week, while a small proportion (6.5%) only recall dreaming one night a week. Almost everyone (80.4%) has had nights when they have recalled more than one dream that night and results were equal regarding when people were most apt to dream, on a weekday or a weekend. Nearly a quarter (24.9%) reported they were more likely to recall their dreams during the week and 22.8% said they were more likely to recall their dreams on the weekend. There are a number of ways in which you can recall your dreams whether it is a weekend or a weekday.

One way to remember dreams is to train yourself to wake up in a leisurely manner, much as you would on a weekend. It is possible to train yourself to wake up automatically by using a clock radio set to classical music. This way, you'll awaken gradually rather than being jolted awake by the harsh buzzing or ringing of an alarm clock. Upon awakening, simply jot down what you remember of your dream or (as some people do) record it on audiotape. Those individuals who are aware of the relevance dreams have to our waking lives, are more likely to recall their dreams. Another way to remember dreams is simply by repeating to yourself at night: "I will remember my dreams, I will remember my dreams."

It is not unusual to recall a dream immediately upon awakening, but by the evening all memories of the dream content has vanished. Absolutely everything we dream is of vital importance; therefore, if we forget even the smallest of details, it can change the meaning of the dream entirely.

There is a common debate as to whether dreams occur in black or white. Research has shown that they occur both in color and black and white. However, when one is in a light state of sleep (as when they first drift off), the dreams are in black and white. Dreams in color occur during the deeper sleep and dream states.

# THREE

## Astral Travel

Astral travel, better known as "OBE's" or "out-of-body experiences" have always been a part of my life. Astral travel is the conscious separation of the astral body from the physical body and as I mentioned, as a child I was under the impression everyone experienced this. However, as I matured I was more hesitant to mention it to people as many of them looked at me as though I had three heads! As well, my husband Thomas, born on the Akwesasne Mohawk reserve, has experienced astral travel since he can remember; however, he too, kept the information to himself for fear people would think he was unbalanced. Finally, one evening he confided in his friend who informed him that there was a whole group of people on the reserve that got together every once in awhile to discuss and compare their out-of-body experiences.

It wasn't until my research on psychic phenomena revealed that Professor Carl Jung, for one, observed activities in his hospital room while in a coma, that I no longer felt alienated from the general population. Like many others who experience astral travel, I could always feel myself leaving my physical body. During one such episode I actually looked down to see myself still lying in bed. It is not unusual for individuals who have had a near-death experience to have later reported observing themselves from above and recalling conversations that took place while they were in such a state...conversations, by the way, that have been verified.

These encounters with the paranormal go a long way in supporting the existence of out-of-body experiences. There are cases on record where an individual (sometimes more than one) actually "sees" the person experiencing the out-of-body experience while at the same time the person experiencing the OBE sees them. Research indicates that approximately 5% to 10% of people have had an out-of-body experience; 85% of them having had the experience while resting comfortably or just prior to sleep (hypnogogic state).

A perfect example of this occurred in my home during the writing of this book. My husband and I were hosts to an overnight guest. At the age of thirty-nine, our guest, Andrew, had never experienced astral travel. Upon awaking the next morning he informed us that he'd had an odd experience after he went to sleep the previous night. He found himself leaving his body and traveling at great speed. His destination? A school auditorium! Oddly enough, I was to attend a "Meet the Teachers" event that evening, but was unable to make it. It appears that Andrew went in my place!

Astral travel allows individuals who experience them a verification of what lies beyond that which we can perceive with our physical senses. The scientists of today are able to utilize far more efficient ontological models and scientific cases by the study and analysis of information from subjects who've experienced lucid OBE's, or out-of-body experiences. Certainly it has been established that every one of us is capable of experiencing the phenomena and the time has finally arrived wherein this universal and long-recognized phenomena is viewed as natural as sleeping and breathing. It is simply a matter of one's consciousness (one's soul) operating separately from the physical body in a spiritual way. Sometimes (as in my case) the individual is aware of the incident, but more often than not retains no memory of the experience.

Certainly references to out-of-body experiences have been documented throughout human history by all civilizations from the most ancient to the most modern, appearing in ancient Egypt between 3,000 and 5,000 years ago. Called the "Ka" by Egyptian priests, the phenomenon was also recorded through the writings of a number of Greek philosophers including Plato and Herodotus, and recorded in the bible as well; for example, in Ezekiel 11.14, the Apocalypse of John 1.10-11 and 4.2 and in the Epistles of Paul of Tarsus, as in 11 Corinthians 12.2.

As a result of the oppression resulting from the Inquisition during the Middle Ages, out-of-body experiences were studied and practiced secretly only within occult or esoteric movements, all information being kept secret from the general populace. It wasn't until the 18th and the 19th centuries that a number of individuals such as Swedish philosopher, Emanuel Swedenborg, French novelist, Honoré de Balzac, and the creator of spiritism, Allan Kardec, gave some credibility to astral travel via their works.

There is absolutely no question that human beings are more than just physical bodies. Speaking from experience I can verify that a lucid out-of-body experience verifies the fact that the physical body is merely a "temporary shelter" through which our consciousness (or awareness) manifests itself merely in the physical dimension. Astral projection generally occurs when the physical body is in what is commonly referred to as the "hypnogogic" state, the state one is in immediately prior to sleep. There is a separation of the nonphysical body from the physical and sometimes (as in my case) the individual is aware of the experience and is able to realize that our self-awareness resides in the nonphysical body as opposed to the physical. The most compelling personal verification of the experience is when the individual retains lucidity outside the body and witnesses his or her physical body still sleeping on the bed.

This type of phenomena occurs as well during an "NDE" (near-death experiences). Literally thousands of documented cases involving accident victims, cardiac arrest patients, et cetera attest to this fact. Commonly referred to as "bilocation," it is acknowledged that our nonphysical bodies are connected to our physical bodies by a retractable field of energy commonly referred to as a "silver cord." (Robert Crookall, *The Study and Practice of Astral Projection,* 1977.) Acting like a leash on our physical body in that it prevents it from getting lost in the outer realms or fails to return to the physical body, the silver cord performs as a intermediary between the physical and spiritual, broken only at the time of biological demise.

At that time, however, the non-physical body, which houses the consciousness, departs to begin a new phase of existence between physical lives. This is termed "the intermissive period." As well, the "silver cord," often referred to as one's bioenergy, or "energetic body" as it is known when the individual is in the physical waking state, is the connection point through which the fields of energy generated by the "chakras" inside our bodies flow back and forth to the non-physical body. This constant exchange of energy is necessary in order to maintain the function of our body, whether in the waking state or outside the physical body, as well as enabling the nonphysical body to travel great distances from its physical counterpart. This bioenergy is also known as vital energy, chi, aura, prana and life force. It emanates from and encompasses every living being as well as ensures a strong connection between the physical and nonphysical bodies, allowing us to experience a rich variety of lucid experiences outside the body. It is possible for us to travel in the physical realm and even visit other dimensions. We can reunite with old friends and acquaintances and even make intelligent decisions.

On a number of occasions I have been asked how one can differentiate between a bona fide out-of-body-experience as opposed to a dream or some other altered state of consciousness provoked by drugs, hormones, medicines, fainting or exhaustion. The answer lies in the fact that a number of characteristics involved in an out-of-body experience clearly distinguish it from a common dream or hallucination. They include:

1.  During an OBE, individuals are lucid, active participants, capable of making decisions and are capable of employing their mental attributes. In dreams, however, one tends to remain passive, having little or no control over the dream experience.

2.  During an OBE, surroundings and situations are real whereas in dreams they are more likely to be distorted or nonsensical.

3.  Situations encountered during an OBE occur independently of the individual's capacity for imagination and creativity.

4.  OBE experiences are more difficult to recall than are dreams simply because the experience occurs beyond the physical brain, and therefore, not recorded by it.

5.  During an OBE, the projector is able to view their physical body, even touch it if they wish, whereas dreams occur inside the physical body.

6.  When one is experiencing an OBE (and I can vouch for this) one has a sense of expanded awareness or euphoria as a result of the ability to fly and pass through physical objects, whereas dreams alone produce more mundane emotions.

6.  An individual experiencing an OBE is able to perceive his or her departure from the extraphysical body from the physical and/or the return of their extraphysical body to the physical.

How does it feel when we leave our physical bodies? The sensations involved in the process of departure, if you will, involve many things. Data has been collected from individuals during courses on OBE's offered around the world by the International Academy of Consciousness, formerly known as The Institute of Projectiology and Conscientiology.

The more common sensations include: falling, floating, projective catalepsy (a sleep paralysis type of sensation), sinking, torpidity (numbness), intracranial sounds (a sound that appears to be coming from inside the head), tingling, clairvoyance, oscillation (a type of swaying or rocking sensation), vibrations and serenity. Other sensations and experiences have been recorded such as the perception of extraphysical beings and various sensations including chills, itching, dramatic temperature changes, tears (watering of the eyes) and not surprisingly, clairvoyance and the tunnel effect. Less common were sensations of spinning, swelling, dizziness, elongation, dematerialization and (believe it or not) bubbling.

## EXAMPLES OF ASTRAL TRAVEL

1.  Self-bilocation—in which the individual perceives him or herself to be in two places at the same time. An example of this is when the subject is able to view his or her physical body whilst manifesting in the extra-physical body.

2.  Often the individual is able to move freely through physical objects such as windows, walls, etc.

3.  Internal autoscopy—wherein the individual has the ability to view his or her internal body including bones and organs together with the consciousness inside the brain.

4.  Cosmoconsciousness—a state of highly expanded awareness in which the individual perceives the order, balance and logic of the universe, simultaneously feeling and celebrating that he or she is part and at one with it. This condition is known by many other names in various fields and religions, including nirvana (Buddhism), satori (Zen Buddhism) and samadhi (Yoga).

5.  Precognition—in which the individual, fully projected from the

physical body, obtains information relating to events that have not yet occurred.

6.  Retrocognition—in which the individual, fully projected from the physical body, obtains information relating to events that have already occurred, most commonly about themselves either from this life or previous lives.

7.  Extraphysical telepathy—in which the projected individual communicates with others who are in the physical, projected or non-physical condition through transmission of thought.

## CURRENT AND HISTORICAL RESEARCH REGARDING ASTRAL TRAVEL

Obviously, personal experimentation is the most logical method of obtaining valid data regarding OBE's, the first being conducted in the U.K. in 1890 by the British Society for Psychical Research. Now, over a hundred years later, a sophisticated online survey analyzing ninety-eight aspects of the OBE was initiated via the Internet by the International Academy of Consciousness.

To date, more than 7,000 individuals have responded and the results show that many characteristics of the phenomena are shared by individuals around the world, irrespective of their age, gender, nationality, ethnicity, cultural background, religion, level of education or socio-economic status. As well, a study was conducted at Oxford University wherein 380 students were asked if they'd ever experienced the sensation of being outside their bodies. Thirty-four per cent of the students answered in the affirmative. In addition, a great deal of research into the phenomena by a number of other scientists has and is still being done.

Janet Lee Mitchell, a researcher at the American Society for Psychical Research in New York, conducted various experiments in order to find answers to the phenomena of "viewing" whilst outside the body.

Ingo Swann, a known surrealist painter and clairvoyant, was chosen as the research subject. As part of the experiment, various objects were placed on a suspended platform above the floor of the room. After "projecting" his vision, Swann described the objects he had viewed, verifying each one in detail. The following year, parapsychologist, Karlis Osis, selected one hundred individuals throughout the United States who were capable of projecting at will, to project themselves out of body and into the premises of the American Society for Psychical Research in New York. Four target objects were placed at a predetermined area inside the building, and although the experiment didn't prove to be a total success, 15% of the participants were able to identify and produce evidence of having been inside the office via astral projection.

Five well-designed experiments have been carried out in Spain, Portugal, the United States and the United Kingdom in which external auditors and judges participated in order to validate the scientific methodology. The results were presented at the third International Congress of Projectiology and Conscientiology at the New York School of Medicine in 2002 and revealed that of the 105 participants, 52 reported 93 cases of an OBE. Oddly enough, the results of that study showed that shapes of objects, followed by colors, are more easily perceived whilst outside the body. It appears that we are not just physical beings, but rather consciousness in evolution.

For example, during an out-of-body experience, the consciousness vacates the physical brain and manifests in the extraphysical body (where our memories of past lives resides.) In this state there is an increased probability of our being able to recall past lives, as well as an increased ability to understand the evolution process such as physical birth, death, and the cycle of lives we have lived.

Having acknowledged that we do not die brings to mind the questions of past and present relationships and possible interconnections between them, as well as the period between lifetimes and the question of what our purpose might be in this particular physical life.

Where do we go when we leave our body? Records from both researchers and conscious projectors have provided a myriad of information regarding this age-old question. Unlike the physical dimension we live in, the extraphysical is made up of many dimensions. The majority of individuals, upon leaving their bodies, however, tend to remain in the dimensional layer closest to the physical dimension, or the earth's crust. It stands to reason that any particular dimension is inhabited by consciousnesses that share the same thoughts and sentiments. In other words, those individuals who are unaware that they are dead (in the biological sense) tend to occupy the same dimension. Then there are the dimensions occupied by communities of evolved consciousnesses who are more than aware of the ongoing cycle of successive lives. These are the ones who have the ability to plan their next physical life that will consist of helping mankind and assisting others with their own evolution.

Everyone on earth experiences some degree of separation from their physical body while in the sleep state, and if one wishes to experience consciousness during astral travel it is imperative that they are able to retain enough lucidity whilst out of the body. This would assist them as well when it came to recalling the experience once back in the physical state. There are various ways to achieve this goal; for example, the room must be dark and free from noise, loose clothing is important as well as being relaxed and in a state of emotional equilibrium. It is important to remain confident of achieving success in the venture and to cast away all doubts and fears. One should avoid certain activities prior to their attempt at experiencing astral travel, activities such as watching films or reading books that contain violent or exciting scenes. Shy completely away from negative thoughts and emotions and above all, do not partake of alcohol or use any drugs. Such mundane things as a full bladder or stomach should also be avoided as the discomfort inhibits the concentration. Keep in mind that provoking astral travel is far easier if one is in a deep, relaxed state, physically tired or in the hypnogogic state (alpha state that occurs just previous to sleep). Above all, mental concentration, determination and a very strong desire cannot be underestimated.

As I mentioned, every human being, without exception, has the capability to project the consciousness from the physical body. If indeed this process is as natural as sleeping and breathing, why is it that ninety-nine percent of humans cannot remember experiencing astral travel? The answer lies in the fact that the majority of individuals leave their bodies with absolutely no awareness or lucidity whatsoever. There are many reasons for this; among them is the fact that there is a common lack of interest in anything other than the physical, an inability to differentiate the out-of-body experience from a common dream and last, but far from least, religious conditioning or brainwashing.

For those who tend to fear such phenomena, it is vital to remember that during a lucid out-of-body experience, one is capable of accessing and applying all capacities they employ whilst in the waking state. For example, memory, decision-making, rationality and critical judgment are not in any way inhibited by the experience.

## TYPES OF OUT-OF-BODY EXPERIENCES

There are numerous types of OBE's. The difference lies in how they occur. For example, the most common type is the "spontaneous" or accidental experience in that the individual had no intention of leaving his or her body, and is often unaware that the phenomena even occurred. By contrast, an "intentional OBE" is planned and carried out by using various projective procedures and techniques. The "confirmed" OBE is when the subject is able to attain enough lucidity outside the body to carry out a specific task thereby enabling him or her to confirm the extraphysical state they are in. An example of this would be seeing something in the physical dimension that can be confirmed at a later date. This is the type of experience that allows scientists to carry on their experimental research on the OBE phenomena.

Most interesting is the OBE experience in which the subject is able to encounter a friend, family member or other acquaintance who has already passed away. Reports of encounters with friends who were also conscious outside their bodies and able to communicate have also been recorded and verified. But without doubt, the most fascinating type of OBE experience is the "continuously conscious" wherein the individual is able to maintain his or her awareness throughout every stage of the experience; in other words, during the period of their normal waking state, their relaxation, the separation of the nonphysical body, the time spent outside the body, the return of the extraphysical body to the physical body and last but far from least, the return to normal waking state (waking up).

Whether we are aware of it, paranormal phenomena is very much a part of our everyday lives. How many times have you felt the need to do something, say something, without knowing exactly why? Many times we fail to recognize that indeed we are experiencing a paranormal phenomena, be it intuition, clairaudience, channeling or clairvoyance. One must keep in mind that our ability to experience such phenomena is merely a normal condition of the consciousness that performs independently of the level of the individual's psychic abilities, or lack thereof, in the normal waking state. Research that allows us to identify and better understand nonphysical dimensions and beings also give us a far better understanding of the true nature of our reality. (One such interesting book is, *Psychic Oddities,* by Hereward Hubert Levington Carrington, 1952.)

The non-physical dimension, however, is so far removed from the physical material existence that during our conscious OBE's we encounter things that are totally foreign to us. For example, when manifesting outside the body, we can fly! We have 360-degree vision, and it isn't unheard of to exit the earth's atmosphere at amazing speeds. As well, the existence of interrelations between the physical and extraphysical dimensions makes it easier to accept the numerous documented cases of phenomena such as ghosts, poltergeists, and the perceived presence of a relative who is deceased, to name just a few.

Those of us who experience lucid OBE's are provided with undeniable personal evidence of life after death. Some may even be privy to their purpose for this life as it was established prior to being born. Recalls of past lives or periods between lives are also revealed. There is no doubt that regular, lucid experiences outside the body greatly enhance an individuals parapsychic abilities and extrasensory perceptions. As well, the more OBE experiences one has, the more he or she is able to develop the exact nature of their interactions with both physical and nonphysical beings, and to communicate directly with those evolved extraphysical beings whose presence is unnoticed by the great majority of the population.

Many societies of the 21$^{st}$ century have matured beyond the unfounded fears and superstitions that may have limited the perspective of their ancestors. As more people around the world have better access to education, ideas, information and the world at large than ever before, they have become increasingly resistant to traditions belonging to bygone eras and are more questioning, critical, discerning and independent in their thinking.

Consistent with this general shift towards transparency, it is possible today to study the out-of-body experience within formal, structured, academic environments. In Brazil, in 1989, for example, a new science, "conscientiology," was proposed for the study of consciousness (individual essence, soul or spirit) with rationality and logic— free of all dogma, rituals and mysticism. This relatively new science takes into account all the attributes of the consciousness, its phenomena (including the out-of-body experience), and the fact that it has multiple lives and can manifest both inside and outside the physical body.

The main premise of conscientiology is participatory research. In other words, researchers, students and all interested individuals are encouraged to have their own experiences and verify the true nature of their existence for themselves by using the OBE as their main research tool. The science of "projectiology" is a sub-discipline of conscientiology, exclusively dedicated to the investigation of the out-of-body experience and related phenomena.

# FOUR

## Near-Death Experiences

Thanks to progress in medical science, a significantly higher percentage of patients are being resuscitated from clinical death, Some of them report surprisingly similar experiences such as traveling through a tunnel, being met by deceased family members or a radiant figure before entering in a heavenly sphere in a state of high and glorious euphoria. As a result of continuing research in the last decades more and more of these experiences are being recorded, analyzed and compared. In exceptional cases some individuals have reported seeing people whom they surmised were still living, but whose death announcement had not reached them as yet.

Former United States President, Bill Clinton, experienced "Death Visions" when surgeons stopped his heart for 73 minutes in order to by pass arteries that were 90% clogged. In short, Clinton was clinically dead.

According to Clinton:

"I saw dark masks crushing, like death masks being crushed, in series," he told the ABC News Primetime Live programme. "Then I'd see these great circles of light. And then, like, Hillary's picture or Chelsea's face would appear on the light, and then they'd fly off into the dark, into the distance. It was amazing."

Dr. Raymond Moody became world famous following the publication of his 1975 best-selling book entitled, *Life After Life*, a veritable treasure trove of information focusing on near-death experiences like never before. Actually, it was Moody himself who coined the term "near-death experience." For the book, Moody recorded and compared the experiences of 150 individuals who died, came very close to death, but then recovered. His research describes the results of decades of inquiry into the NDE phenomenon. According to his extensive research there are nine elements that commonly occur during a near-death experience:

1. Strange sounds: A buzzing or ringing sound while having a sense of being dead.

2. Peace without pain: When an individual is dying they are apt to be in a great deal of pain, but once they leave their bodies the pain vanishes and they experience a beautiful sense of peace.

3. Out-of-body experience: A sensation of rising up and floating, a sense of being in a spiritual body, or sometimes the individual finds themselves floating above their own bodies and feeling comfortable while they view their body below, surrounded by a medical team.

4. The tunnel experience: A sense of being drawn into darkness through a tunnel at an extremely high speed, until reaching a radiant golden-white light. Though the individuals often report feeling

afraid, they do not sense that they were on their way to hell.

5. Rising rapidly into the heavens: Some individuals report rising directly and suddenly rising into the heavens and seeing the earth and the celestial sphere, as they would be had they been astronauts in space.

6. People of Light: Following their arrival on the other side of the tunnel, or after they have risen into the heavens, the dying meet people who glow with an inner light. Often they find friends and relatives who have already died are there to greet them.

7. The Being of Light: After meeting the people of light, the dying often meet a powerful spiritual being whom some have identified as God, Jesus, or some religious figure.

8. The Life Review: The Being of Light presents the dying with a panoramic review of everything they have ever done. In other words, they relive every act they have ever done to other people, and come away feeling that love is the most important thing in life.

9. Reluctance to return: The Being of Light tells the dying that they must return to life. Other times, they are given a choice of staying or returning. In either case, they are always reluctant to return. The individuals who do choose to return do so only because of loved ones they do not wish to leave behind.

In his book, Dr. Moody elaborates on the "Being of Light" observed by those who have experienced near death:

What is perhaps the most incredible common element in the accounts I have studied, and one that has the most profound effect upon the individual, is the encounter with a very bright light. Typically, at it's first appearance this light is dim, but it rapidly gets brighter until it reaches an unearthly brilliance. Yet, even though this light (usually said to be white or "clear") is of an indescribable brilliance, many make the specific point that it does not in any way hurt their eyes, or dazzle them, or keep them from seeing other things around them (perhaps because at this point they don't have physical "eyes" to be dazzled.) Despite the light's unusual manifestation, however, not one person has expressed any doubt whatsoever that it was a being, a being, of light. Not only that, it has a very definite personality. The love and warmth which emanate from this being to the dying person are utterly beyond words, and he feels completely surrounded by it and taken up in it, completely at ease and accepted in the presence of this being. He senses an irresistible magnetic attraction to this light.

Interestingly, while the above description of the Being of Light is utterly invariable, the identification of the being varies from individual to individual, and seems to be largely a function of the religious background, training, or beliefs of the person involved. Thus, most of those who are Christians in training or belief identify the light as Christ and sometimes draw Biblical parallels in support of their interpretation. A Jewish man and woman identified the light as an "angel." It was clear though, in both cases, that the subjects did not mean to imply that the being had wings, played a harp, or even had a human shape or appearance. There was only the light. What each was trying to get across was that they took the being to be an emissary or a guide. A man who had no religious beliefs or training at all prior to his experience simply identified what he saw as "a being of light." One lady of the Christian faith, who apparently did not feel any compulsion at all to call it "Christ," used the same label.

Shortly after its appearance, the being begins to communicate with the person who is passing over. Notably, this communication is of the same direct kind which we encountered earlier in the description of how a person in the spiritual body may "pick up the thoughts" of those around him for—here again—people claim that they did not hear any physical voice or sounds coming from the being, nor did they respond to the being through audible sounds. Rather, it is reported that a direct, unimpeded transfer of thoughts takes place, and in such a clear way that there is no possibility whatsoever either of misunderstanding or of flying to the light. Furthermore, this unimpeded exchange does not even take place in the native language of the person. Yet, he understands perfectly and is instantaneously aware. He cannot even translate the thoughts and exchanges that took place while he was near death into the human language that he must speak now, after his resuscitation.

The next step of the experience clearly illustrates the difficulty of translating from this unspoken language. The being almost immediately directs a certain thought to the person to whose presence it has come so dramatically. Usually the persons to whom I have talked try to formulate the thought into a question. Among the translations I have heard are: "Are you prepared to die?" "Are you ready to die?" "What have you done with your life to show me?" and "What have you done with your life that is sufficient?"

The first two formulations that stress "preparation" might at first seem to have a different sense from the second pair, which emphasizes "accomplishment." However, some support for my own feeling that everybody is trying to express the same thought comes from the narrative of one woman who put it this way: "The first thing he said to me, that he kind of asked me, was if I was ready to die, or, what I had done with my life that I feel I wanted to show him."

One man told me that during his "death," the voice asked him a question: "Is it worth it?" And what it meant was—was the kind of life I had been leading up to that point seem worthwhile to me then, knowing what I then knew."

Incidentally, all insist that this question, ultimate and profound as it may be in its emotional impact, is not at all asked in condemnation. The being, all seem to agree, does not direct the question to them to accuse or threaten them, for they still feel the total love and acceptance coming from the light, no matter what their answer may be. Rather, the point of the question seems to be to make them think about their lives, to draw them out. It is, if you will, a Socratic question, one asked not to acquire information but to help the person who is being asked to proceed along the path to the truth by himself.

Let us look at some firsthand accounts of this fantastic being:

1. "I heard the doctors say that I was dead, and that's when I began to feel as though I were tumbling, actually kind of floating, through this blackness, which was some kind of enclosure. There are not really words to describe this. Everything was very black, except that, way off from me, I could see this light. It was a very, very, brilliant light, but not too large at first. It grew larger as I came nearer and nearer to it. I was trying to get to that light at the end, because I felt it was Christ, and I was trying to reach that point. It was not a frightening experience. It was more or less a pleasant thing. For immediately, being a Christian, I had connected with the light with Christ, who said, 'I am the light of the world.' I said to myself: *If this is it, if I am to die, then I know who waits for me at the end, there in that light.*"

2. "I got up and walked into the hall to go get a drink, and it was at that point, as they found out later, that my appendix ruptured. I became very weak and I fell down. I began to feel a sort of drifting, a movement of my real being in and out of my body, and to hear beautiful music. I floated on down the hall and out the door onto the screened-in porch. There, it almost seemed that clouds, a pink mist really, began to gather around me, and then I floated right straight on through the screen, just as though it weren't there, and up into this pure crystal-clear light, an illuminating white light. It was beautiful and so bright, so radiant, but it didn't hurt my eyes. It's not any kind of light you can describe on earth. I didn't actually see a person in this light, and yet it has a special identity, it definitely does. It is a light of perfect understanding and perfect love. The thought came to my mind, 'Lovest thou me?' This was

not exactly in the form of a question, but I guess the connotation of what the light said was, 'If you do love me, go back and complete what you began in your life.' And all during this time, I felt as though I were surrounded by an overwhelming love and compassion."

3. "I knew I was dying and there was nothing I could do about it, because no one could hear me…I was out of my body, there's no doubt about it, because I could see my own body there on the operation room table. My soul was out! All this made me feel very bad at first, but then, this really bright light came. It did seem that it was a little dim at first, but then it was this huge beam. It was just a tremendous amount of light, nothing like a big, bright flashlight, it was just too much light. And it gave off heat to me; I felt a warm sensation. It was a bright yellowish white—more white. It was tremendously bright; I just can't describe it. It seemed that it covered everything, yet it didn't prevent me from seeing everything around me: the operating room, the doctors and nurses—everything. I could see clearly, and it wasn't blinding. At first, when the light came, I wasn't sure what was happening, but then, it asked, it kind of asked me if I was ready to die. It was like talking to a person, but a person wasn't there. The light's what was talking to me, but in a voice. Now, I think that the voice that was talking to me actually realized that I wasn't ready to die. You know, it was just kind of testing me more than anything else. Yet, from the moment the light spoke to me, I felt really good—secure and loved. The love which came from it is just unimaginable, indescribable. It was a fun person to be with! And it had a sense of humor, too—definitely!"

"Dying is an integral part of life, as natural and predictable as being born. But whereas birth is cause for celebration, death has become a dreaded and unspeakable issue to be avoided by every means possible in our modern society. Perhaps it is that in spite of all our technological advances. We may be able to delay it, but we cannot escape it. We, no less than other, non-rational animals, are destined to die at the end of our lives. And death strikes indiscriminately—it cares not at all for the status or position of the ones it chooses; everyone must die, whether rich or poor, famous or unknown. Even good deeds will not exclude their doers from the sentence of death; the good die as often as the bad. It is perhaps this inevitable and unpredictable quality that makes death so frightening to many people. Especially those who put a high value on being in control of their own existence are offended by the thought that they too are subject to the forces of death."

Elisabeth Kübler-Ross

Dr. Elisabeth Kübler-Ross was a Swiss-born psychiatrist and author who gained international fame for her landmark work on death and dying. Named one of the "100 Most Important Thinkers" of the past century by *Time* magazine in 1999, Kübler-Ross was recognized as one of the leading authorities in the fascinating and controversial field of death, dying and transition. It's been said that she was responsible for creating this field of research. Kübler-Ross died at the age of seventy-eight, leaving behind a legacy of her works including among them several books: *On Death and Dying, Life Lessons* and *On Life After Death,* the latter containing a collection of informative and in-depth material she had acquired throughout the years working with the dying. Following, is an excerpt from the book in which she describes one of the most fascinating near-death experiences she has encountered:

My most dramatic and unforgettable case of "ask and you will be given," and also of an NDE, was a man who was in the process of being picked up by his entire family for a Memorial

Day weekend drive to visit some relatives out of town. While driving in the family van to pick him up, his parents-in-law with his wife and eight children were hit by a gasoline tanker. The gasoline poured over the car and burned his entire family to death. After being told what happened, this man remained in a state of total shock and numbness for several weeks. He stopped working and was unable to communicate. To make a long story short, he became a total bum, drinking half-a-gallon of whisky a day, trying heroin and other drugs to numb his pain. He was unable to hold a job for any length of time and ended up literally in the gutter.

It was during one of my hectic traveling tours, having just finished the second lecture in a day on life after death, that a hospice group in Santa Barbara asked me to give yet another lecture. After my preliminary statements, I became aware that I am very tired of repeating the same stories over and over again. And I quietly said to myself: *Oh God, why don't you send me somebody from the audience who has had a NDE and is willing to share it with the audience so I can take a break? They will have a first-hand experience instead of hearing my old stories over and over again.*

At that very moment the organizer of the group gave me a little slip of paper with an urgent message on it. It was a message from a man from the bowery who begged to share his NDE with me. I took a little break and sent a messenger to his bowery hotel. A few moments later, after a speedy cab ride, the man appeared in the audience. Instead of being a bum as he had described himself, he was a rather well dressed, very sophisticated man. He went up on the stage and without having a need to evaluate him, I encouraged him to tell the audience what he needed to share. He told how he had been looking forward to the weekend family reunion, how his entire family had piled into a family van and were on the way to pick him up when this tragic accident occurred which burned his entire family to death. He shared the shock and the numbness, the utter disbelief of suddenly being a single man, of having had children and suddenly becoming childless, of living without a single close relative. He told of his total inability to come to grips with it. He shared how he changed from a money-earning, decent, middle-class husband and father to a total bum, drunk every day from morning to night, using every conceivable drug and trying to commit suicide in every conceivable way, yet he was never able to succeed. His last recollection was that after two years of literally bumming around, he was lying on a dirt road at the edge of a forest, drunk and stoned as he called it, trying desperately to be reunited with his family. Not wanting to live, not even having the energy to move out of the road when he saw a big truck coming toward him and running over him.

It was at this moment that he watched himself in the street, critically injured, while he observed the whole scene of the accident from a few feet above. It was at this moment that his family appeared in front of him, in a glow of light with an incredible sense of love. They had happy smiles on their faces, and simply made him aware of their presence, not communicating in any verbal way but in the form of thought transference, sharing with him the joy and happiness of their present existence.

This man was not able to tell us how long this reunion lasted. He was so awed by his family's health, their beauty, their radiance and their total acceptance of this present situation, by their unconditional love. He made a vow not to touch them, not to join them, but to re-enter his physical body so that he could share with the world what he had experienced. It would be a form of redemption for his two years of trying to throw his physical life away. It was after this vow that he watched the truck driver carry his totally injured body into the car. He saw an ambulance speeding to the scene of the accident, he was taken to the hospital's emergency room and he finally re-entered his physical body, tore off the straps that were tied around him and literally walked out of the emergency room. He never had delirium tremens or any after-effects from the heavy abuse of drugs and alcohol. He felt healed and whole, and made a commitment that he would not die until he had the opportunity of sharing the existence of life after death with as many people as would be willing to listen. It was after reading a newspaper article about my appearance in Santa Barbara that he sent a message to the auditorium.

By allowing him to share with my audience he was able to keep the promise he made at the time of his short, temporary, yet happy reunion with his entire family.

We do not know what happened to this man since then, but I will never forget the glow in his eyes, the joy and deep gratitude he experienced, that he was led to a place where, without doubt and questioning, he was allowed to stand up on the stage and share with a group of hundreds of hospice workers the total knowledge and awareness that our physical body is only the shell that encloses our immortal self.

According to Elisabeth Kübler-Ross:

And after your death, when most of you for the first time

realize what life here is all about, you will begin to see that your life here is almost nothing but the sum total of every choice you have made during every moment of your life. Your thoughts, which you are responsible for, are as real as your deeds. You will begin to realize that every word and every deed affects your life and has also touched thousands of lives.

As far as service goes, it can take the form of a million things. To do service, you don't have to be a doctor working in the slums for free, or become a social worker. Your position in life and what you do doesn't matter as much as how you do what you do.

Death is simply a shedding of the physical body like the butterfly shedding its cocoon. It is a transition to a higher state of consciousness where you continue to perceive, to understand, to laugh, and to be able to grow. Dying is nothing to fear. It can be the most wonderful experience of your life. It all depends on how you have lived. For those who seek to understand it, death is a highly creative force. The highest spiritual values of life can originate from the thought and study of death. Guilt is perhaps the most painful companion of death.

How do the geese know when to fly to the sun? Who tells them the seasons? How do we, humans, know when it is time to move on? As with the migrant birds, so surely with us, there is a voice within, if only we would listen to it, that tells us so certainly when to go forth into the unknown. I believe that we are solely responsible for our choices, and we have to accept the consequences of every deed, word, and thought throughout our lifetime. I didn't fully realize it at the time, but the goal of my life was profoundly molded by this experience—to help produce, in the next generation, more Mother

Teresas and less Hitlers. I say to people who care for people who are dying, if you really love that person and want to help them, be with them when their end comes close. Sit with them—you don't even have to talk. It is not the end of the physical body that should worry us. Rather, our concern must be to live while we're alive—to release our inner selves from the spiritual death that comes with living behind a facade designed to conform to external definitions of who and what we are. It's only when we truly know and understand that we have a limited time on earth—and that we have no way of knowing when our time is up, we will then begin to live each day to the fullest, as if it was the only one we had. I've told my children that when I die, to release balloons in the sky to celebrate that I graduated. For me, death is a graduation. Learn to get in touch with silence within yourself and know that everything in life has a purpose. Live so you do not have to look back and say: "God, how I have wasted my life."

People are like stained-glass windows. They sparkle and shine when the sun is out, but when the darkness sets in, their true beauty is revealed only if there is a light from within. Should you shield the valleys from the windstorms, you would never see the beauty of their canyons. The most beautiful people we have known are those who have known defeat, known suffering, known struggle, known loss, and have found their way out of the depths. These persons have an appreciation, sensitivity and an understanding of life that fills them with compassions, gentleness, and a deep loving concern. Beautiful people do not just happen.

The ultimate lesson all of us have to learn is unconditional love, which includes not only others but ourselves as well. There is no joy without hardship. If not for death, would we appreciate life? If not for hate, would we know the ultimate goal is love?...At these moments you can either hold on to negativity or look for blame, or you can choose to heal and keep on loving. There is no need to go to India or anywhere else to find peace. You will find that deep place of silence right in your room, your garden or even your bathtub. Those who learned to know death, rather than to fear and fight it, become our teachers about life.

Throughout life, we get clues that remind us of the direction we are supposed to be headed...if you stay focused, then you learn your lessons. Watching a peaceful death of a human being reminds us of a falling star; one of a million lights in a vast sky that flares up for a brief moment only to disappear into the endless night forever. We have to ask ourselves whether medicine is to remain a humanitarian and respected profession or a new but depersonalized science in the service of prolonging life rather than diminishing human suffering.

We make progress in society only if we stop cursing and complaining about its shortcomings and have the courage to do something about them. We need to teach the next generation of children from day one that they are responsible for their lives. Mankind's greatest gift, also its greatest curse, is that we have free choice. We can make our choices built from love or from fear. We run after values that, at death, become zero. At the end of your life, nobody asks you how many degrees you have, or how many mansions you built, or how many Rolls Royces you could afford. That's what dying patients teach you. When we have passed the tests we are sent to Earth to learn, we are allowed to graduate. We are allowed to shed our body, which imprisons our souls...When you learn your lessons, the pain goes away.

You will not grow if you sit in a beautiful flower garden, but you will grow if you are sick, if you are in pain, if you experience losses, and if you do not put your head in the sand, but take the pain as a gift to you with a very, very specific purpose. Instead, the goal of life becomes not to elude death— but, because one's fears do not center so much on it, rather to live in concert with it. After an NDE, the survivor finds a new lease on life. She/he is more willing to try new things and to fit as many things as possible into it because she/he is no longer so afraid of what will happen at death. After the NDE, life is more cherished, and the relationships that gave that life more meaning are emphasized upon. The NDE encourages growth and exploration; its acknowledgment helps for those in a society to desire continued testing of the limits and possibilities of life.

I've told my children that when I die, to release balloons in the sky to celebrate that I graduated. For me, death is a graduation.

Dr. Elisabeth Kübler-Ross

Dr. Edgar Cayce was a man who, over the span of his lifetime (1877 to 1945), experienced more near-death experiences than anyone ever documented. Using hypnosis to induce a near-death experience, Cayce made over 14,000 journeys into the spirit realm and was able to access virtually unlimited information by visiting the so-called "Hall-of Records" described by a large number of near-death experiences. He learned that when he was hypnotized, he would leave his body and journey into the afterlife realms. The information he gained from these journeys have astounded people from all over the world. In 1910, the *New York Times* carried two pages of headlines and pictures in which he was declared the "World's Most Mysterious Man." A national magazine ran an article titled, "Miracle Man of Virginia Beach" and Cayce was literally swamped with an avalanche of 25,000 requests for medical help.

In 1954, the University of Chicago accepted a Ph.D. thesis based on a study of his life and work. Cayce is also considered to be the father of holistic medicine by *Journal of the American Medical Association (JAMA),* the prestigious medical journal. Cayce was a wonder to the medical community because of his ability to diagnose and specify treatment for gravely ill people, often hundreds of miles away through his out-of-body journeys. Cayce was able to gain a tremendous amount of information through his frequent NDE's. Much of this information solved some of the greatest mysteries of humanity.

Cayce revealed that his subconscious mind (which he identified as the "soul") would leave his body and explore the dimension where all subconscious minds are connected—a dimension similar in description to Carl Jung's Collective Unconsciousness. It is the realm of thought, imagination, dreams, after-death, and near-death states where all things are possible. Though Casey didn't experience clinical or brain death, he was capable of controlling his mind in order to travel consciously through the exact same process as the near-death state. According to Casey, anyone is capable of doing the same provided the proper attunement is made. Actually, this is done by everyone when they fall asleep and enter the realm of dreams, the difference being it is then done sub-consciously as opposed to consciously. The same principle applies to death.

On three separate occasions he went on record to describe his out-of-body journeys to the public. The following is the only waking description of his journey in the trance state, taken verbatim from comments he made at a public lecture:

> I see myself as a tiny dot out of my physical body, which
> lies inert before me. I find myself oppressed by darkness and

there is a feeling of terrific loneliness. Suddenly I am conscious of a white beam of light, knowing that I must follow it or be lost. As I move along this path of light, I gradually become conscious of various levels upon which there is movement. Upon the first level there are vague, horrible shapes, grotesque forms such as one sees in nightmares. Passing on, there begins to appear, on either side, misshapen forms of human beings with some part of the body magnified. Again there is change and I become conscious of gray-hooded forms moving downward. Gradually, these become lighter in color. Then the direction changes and these forms move upward and the color of the robes grow rapidly lighter. Next, there begins to appear on either side, vague outlines of houses, walls, trees etc., but everything is motionless. As I pass on there is more light and movement in what appears to be normal cities and towns. With the growth of movement I begin to become conscious of sounds, at first, indistinct rumblings, then music, laughter and singing of birds. There is more and more light. The colors become very beautiful and there is the sound of wonderful music. The houses are left behind; ahead there is only a blending of sound and color.

## SCIENTIFIC THEORIES OF THE NEAR-DEATH EXPERIENCE

*Death's Door* (Dell, 1996) is an excellent book written by Jean Ritchie, in which she describes all the theories explaining the near-death experience:

It is important to realize the fact that although the mechanism for the dying process in the brain can be quantified, this by no means proves that NDE's are merely a vision produced by the brain which ends upon permanent brain death. Science is unable to prove this because of the large amount of circumstantial evidence that consciousness can exist far removed from the body. In the same vein, science cannot prove that consciousness can survive death; however, research is underway right now that may provide scientific evidence that consciousness can exist outside the body. Many people, such as myself, believe it is only a matter of time. NDE researchers do not have to prove anything. The circumstantial evidence is in their favor. But science has a lot of explaining to do if it tries to claim the consciousness does not survive death. A good analogy of one current theory of consciousness assumes that consciousness is not localized in the skull.

Assuming consciousness is like a television signal that exists in the airwaves and is being processed by a television set (the brain) to produces images on the screen (brain chemistry) representing a television program (a near-death experience.) Using this analogy, current scientific theories claim that the near-death experience is a product of the television set. In other words, the television program is a product of the television set. Using the analogy, this would be false because it is the television signal working with the television that produces the television program. Some scientific claims state that death is the end of consciousness—like shutting off the television set is the end of the television signal in the airwaves. Using this analogy, you can see that such a statement is false. Shutting off the television does not affect the television signal in the airwaves.

There exists a scientific theory stating that near-death experiences are indeed memories of birth and have nothing whatsoever to do with death. During birth, an infant leaves the womb and travels down a tunnel toward the light. The infant then finds that the light is a place which holds a great deal of love and warmth. This theory states that at the point of death, the stored memory of birth emerges. There are, however, numerous discrepancies in this theory. Firstly, during birth, the baby, rather than floating at high speed down a tunnel, is pushed along with much difficulty by it's mother's contractions.

Then too, how does this theory explain the happy reunions with friends and relatives who have predeceased us? The theory also suggests that the "Being of Light" is actually the doctor or midwife assisting in the birth, however, an infant's nervous system is not sufficiently developed to allow it to assimilate and store any memories of the birth experience. One could also argue that the feelings of peace and bliss are simply memories of the security of the womb, an existence far removed from stresses and anxieties, but what about the same feelings one experiences upon being relieved of pain and suffering at the point of death? How about the infant whose birth experience, [such as mine], rather than being pleasant, is filled with agonizing pain? As opposed to a near-death experience, which is commonly described as the most pleasurable experience an individual can have, some births are terribly unpleasant.

# FIVE

## Reincarnation

*"The tomb is not a blind alley; it is a thoroughfare.*
*It closes on the twilight. It opens on the dawn."*

*Victor Hugo*

Have you ever experienced a strong sense of "déjà vu," a certainty that you've been there? Done that? Heard that? Said that? According to a recent Gallup poll, belief in reincarnation has increased from 21% to 25% over the last decade. It is believed that Benjamin Franklin was professing his belief in reincarnation when he wrote that he would return "in a new and more elegant edition, revised and corrected by the author." General George S. Patton believed that he had been a soldier in many previous lives, including in the service of Alexander the Great. Thomas Edison and Henry Ford were contemporaries and both professed believers in past lives. The great American psychic, Edgar Cayce, was of the belief that he was a one-time resident of Atlantis. Actor, Glen Ford, relived five past lives while under hypnosis. Shaken by the experience of the regressions he said: "It conflicts with all my religious beliefs. I'm a God-fearing man and proud of it, but this has got me mixed up."

Psychiatrist Dr. Ian Stevenson does not believe that genetics alone, or combined with environmental influences, can explain the various peculiarities and abnormalities of human personalities that are evident to psychiatrists. "I think a rational person can believe in reincarnation on the basis of the evidence," says Dr. Stevenson who believes the possibility of reincarnation illuminates the inexplicable behavior that occurs very early in a person's life and continues until their demise. This is behavior unheard of in the individual's family; therefore, genetics or imitation from a family member fails to explain it.

For over forty years Dr. Stevenson has scrutinized more than 3,000 cases in which children—generally between the ages of two and five—describe their former lives at the same time they learn to speak. Focusing his studies on children simply because their accounts are far less likely to be tainted than some adults who lay claim to former lives, the youngsters are extremely specific in terms of their former names, relatives, the towns they lived in, and even their lovers names. In one case, a girl recalled dying after being hit by a car when she was in her teens. She said her name had been Sheila. Arrangements were made for Sheila's siblings and parents to meet her, and according to eyewitnesses, she knew all their names without ever having met them in this lifetime.

Worthy of note is the fact that in terms of memories from past lives, it appears that children in India are far more likely to give specific details concerning their former lives, often as many as twenty or thirty details including proper names. According to Dr. Stevenson, a large percentage of American children who recall previous lives are unable to recall many specific details and as a result there remain a large number of "unsolved cases." In India, the percentage of "unsolved cases" is only about 20 percent.

"In cases of reincarnation," declares Stevenson, "I have to use the methods of the historian, lawyer and psychiatrist. I gather testimony from as many witnesses as possible. It is not uncommon for me to interview twenty-five people in regard to one case of reincarnation. I have frequently gone back to interview the same people several years later."

In 1988, *Omni* magazine said of Stevenson: "His studies are scrupulously objective and methodologically impeccable." A 1975 article in *The Journal of the American Medical Association (JAMA)* said that Stevenson "had collected cases in which the evidence is difficult to explain on any other grounds [other than reincarnation]."

Certainly in terms of sexual disorders there is much evidence wherein an individual whom we would term "transsexual" truly believe they are of the opposite sex. Their mode of dress and behavior is that of the opposite sex. A significant number of these transsexuals, many of whom live in the West, often endure surgical procedures in order to alter their physical transsexual self—and this appears to have its roots in geographical areas. For example, tribes in Northwest America and people in Lebanon and Turkey don't believe that such a thing as a "sex-change" is possible and there are no reported cases of this type whatsoever. Thailand boasts of 16 percent of sex change operations. Burma's incidence is 25 percent and India, as in the majority of cases worldwide, is 5 percent.

Though Stevenson's work is fully accepted in all Eastern societies, in our own society, any reference to reincarnation is met with extreme skepticism, especially from logic-brained, linear thinkers. According to Bertrand Russell, "Most people would rather die than think; in fact, they do so."

Ian Stevenson was born in Montréal on Halloween Day, 1918, just 11 days before the Treaty of Versailles was signed to end World War I. His father became the chief Ottawa correspondent for the *Times* of

London; his mother held an impressive library of esoterica. Stevenson studied medicine at the University of St. Andrews in Scotland but returned to Montréal to continue his studies at McGill. As a doctor of medicine he became interested in psychosomatic illnesses, which lead him into Freudian psychoanalysis. In 1957, Stevenson was appointed chief psychiatrist at the hospital of the University of Virginia, where, to this day, he heads the Division of Personality Studies. Stevenson's special area of study has been evidence for survival, and apparent memories of former lives, all of which led to the publication of his book, *Twenty Cases Suggestive of Reincarnation*. In 1960, he published his first essay on reincarnation, "The Evidence for Survival from Claimed Memories of Former Incarnations." That essay caught the attention of Chester Carlson, the man who invented the Xerox machine. So impressed with Stevenson's work, Carlson bequeathed a chair at the University of Virginia with funding in excess of one million dollars in order that the field of research could continue.

Abandoning his psychiatric studies in 1964, Stevenson has, with a great deal of assistance from his friend Carlson, continued his research into psychic phenomena and reincarnation. He has since scoured the world in his search for evidence of reincarnation and in the late 60's was logging in excess of 50,000 miles a year, traveling to and fro, from North America to India, Sri Lanka and countries throughout the Mid and Far East.

Cynics are quick to point out that the majority of cases that Stevenson offers as evidence of reincarnation derive from areas where the main religions advocate Reincarnation. Stevenson's response to these critics is simple: if parents in the West were more accepting of the idea of reincarnation they would be more sensitive to their children's stories which they dismiss as the ramblings of overactive imaginations. As well, Stevenson goes on to explain that Christian theologians have all but strangled the life out of the idea of reincarnation in the West in spite of the fact it has roots on this side of the planet.

According to Stevenson: "Some Southern European Christians

believed in reincarnation until the Council of Nice banned such beliefs in 533 AD. Shopenhauer took it seriously and Voltaire's observations that it is no more surprising to be born twice than once is well known." He adds, "In the Republic, Plato describes souls about to be reborn as choosing their former lives."

Stevenson continues, by adding that: "cases of the reincarnation type suggest that although personality is indeed formed in childhood, its development actually begins much earlier in other terrestrial lives anterior to the present life. If we allow ourselves to think of the formation of human personality as extending further back in time than conception and birth, we may be able to explain better than we now can a number of anomalies in child development and human personality for which, up until now, theorists have had to invent 'epicyclical' addenda to their theories that simply increase their top-heaviness and suggest that they have overlooked some additional essential component."

The most convincing cases that Stevenson has discovered are those that include physical evidence of reincarnation. Stevenson published an article in an academic journal in 1993 in which he states that in the cases he studied of children claiming past lives, (he has compiled over 3,000 cases, but has only been able to seriously examine a small percentage of them 309 to be precise, or 35%) have birth- marks or birth defects that correspond with physical abnormalities attributed to the previous personality (most of which are thought to be wounds left as a result of some sort of violent event that terminated the life of the previous personality).

"In cases in which a deceased person was identified, the details of whose life unmistakably matched the child's statements, a close correspondence was nearly always found between the birthmarks and/or birth defects on the child and the wounds on the deceased person." Stevenson further states that, "in 43 of the 49 cases in which a medical document (usually a post-mortem report) was obtained, it confirmed the correspondence between wounds and birthmarks (or birth defects)."

In one such case, an Indian boy was born with a curious circular set of birthmarks on his chest. The birthmarks almost perfectly matched the drawings from an autopsy report of the shotgun wounds that ended the life of a man that was killed fifteen years prior to the boy's birth in a village thirty kilometers away. The boy told vividly detailed stories of the man's life, which included his name.

In another case, a Thai boy was born with a skin defect on his scalp, which corresponded with the knife wound that ended the life of his uncle whom the boy claimed to be reincarnated from. Another Thai boy was born with a birthmark on his scalp that corresponds with the bullet wound left behind on a man whose life he claims to have remembered.

A Turkish boy is born with a deformed ear. He claims to remember the life of a man who was killed by a shotgun blast to the side of the head. The stories go on and on, but still Stevenson has his detractors.

"Why do mainstream scientists refuse to accept the evidence we have for reincarnation?" Stevenson asks somewhat rhetorically, but mostly with an air of complete frustration. Stevenson, now in his eighties, will soon get the answers to all the rest of his questions. Who knows? He may even get the acclaim and respect he deserves in his next incarnation. "There's an old saying: "Science only changes one funeral at a time," Stevenson once told an interviewer while in a very bleak frame of mind.

As we sit at the dawning of the age of information and communication, more and more people feel comfortable exploring subjects that were thought taboo until recently. This intellectual emancipation has resulted in an orgy of enquiry as curious minds sample the fruits that had been hidden, or forbidden, to them by the proverbial powers-that-be. What is commonly referred to as New Age spiritualism has produced a galaxy of stars and superstars, some surely charlatans, others quite possibly prophets, but few, if any, have put together a solid a case for their theories as has Stevenson. In spite of this, Stevenson continues to toil in relative obscurity. He is scoffed at by his scientific peers, but has virtual messiah status with the intelligentsia of New Agers. The thoughts of the professional agnostics who have heard of Stevenson and considered what he has to say are best summed up by Dr. Harold Leif, who wrote in *The Journal of Nervous and Mental Diseases:* "Either he is making a colossal mistake or he will be known as the Galileo of the twentieth century."

How else does one explain the "genius" phenomenon? According to Henry Ford: "Genius is experience. Some seem to think that it is a gift or talent, but it is the fruit of long experience in many lives. Some are older souls than others, and so they know more."

There is no question that reincarnation is of assistance in explaining one's present characteristics, likes, dislikes, talents, fears, et cetera. Over the years I have regressed numerous individuals, and as a result, there is no doubt in my mind that we experience many lifetimes. How else does one explain the genius of someone like the famous composer of the eighteenth century, Wolfgang Amadeus Mozart who, at four years of age, wrote minuets, a piano concerto and a sonata? His compositions at this age were not only technically accurate, but also extremely difficult. At age seven he composed a full-length opera. Another genius, Jean Louis Cardiac, born in 1719 was able to repeat the alphabet when he was just three months old! At three years he was able to read Latin and at four he could translate the language into either English or French. He passed away in Paris at the age of seven.

Basically, reincarnation is the belief that we go through a series of lifetimes for the sole purpose of spiritual growth and soul development. Edgar Cayce's approach, however, doesn't include the concept of transmigration, which states that it is possible for human beings to be born again as animals. From Cayce's point of view, souls only occupy human bodies through their spiritual growth and developmental process. In other words, Cayce's approach to reincarnation provides a philosophical setting to the past focusing on practical ways of dealing with the present life; living, growing, and being of service to one another in the present. For Cayce, it wasn't as important who the individual had been, or even what they had been doing, as it was paramount that they focus on the present and the opportunities and challenges that faced them in this time, this place—right now.

In terms of recalling our own past lives, the Edgar Cayce information provides a vast array of approaches. In fact, oftentimes individuals who received readings would enquire about such things as memorable dreams that were on their mind, personal traits and talents that they have often been drawn to, as well as intense positive or negative relationships with others in their lives. Cayce described how each of these things could be tied to past-life memories. With this in mind, in order to recall your own past lives the Cayce readings recommend such things as personal inventories of your talents, ambitions, abilities, likes and dislikes; working with meditation and dreams; taking part in imaginative past-life reveries or self-hypnosis and so forth.

From Cayce's perspective, the reason for believing in reincarnation is not so that we can dwell upon the past or brag about the possibility of once having been someone famous, instead it is to enable a soul to understand the consequences of previous choices and to know that each individual is ultimately responsible for shaping and creating his or her life in the present. From the Cayce's readings' perspective, the past merely provided a framework of potentials and probabilities. An individual's choices, actions, and free will in the present would determine the actual experience lived this time around. Rather than being a fatalistic approach to life, it is much more one of nearly limitless opportunities.

Dr. Thomas Verny, a Toronto psychiatrist who is not given to metaphysical speculation, writes in his book, *The Secret Life of the Unborn Child,* how the animated faces of researchers in Seattle, Washington, were imitated by a nursery full of babies—some of whom were only one hour old! According to Verny, "When the researcher stuck out his or her tongue, made a face or wiggled fingers in front of a baby, the child often responded in kind." This (and other experiments like it) demonstrates conclusively, he goes on to say, the presence of well-developed thinking, including the handling of abstract ideas in the new-born.

Dr. Ian Stevenson likens reincarnational memory to the effect of carbon paper: when the top copy (the body) is destroyed, the image remains. As well, the data gleaned from past-life regressions tend to confirm the concept of group reincarnation. In other words, the same people are encountered again and again in a variety of bodily disguises. As we continue through our numerous incarnations, even though we assume new roles, we are still surrounded by the same souls.

Dr. Stevenson has collected thousands of cases of children who spontaneously (without hypnosis) recall a past life. He is able to offer convincing scientific evidence for reincarnation. In each case of children's past life memory, he methodically documents the person the child remembers being and verifies the facts of the deceased person's life that match the child's memory. He even matches birthmarks and birth defects to wounds and scars on the deceased, verified by medical records. His strict methods systematically rule out all possible "normal" explanations for the child's memories.

Dr. Stevenson has devoted the last forty years to the scientific documentation of past-life memories of children from all over the world. Many people, including skeptics and scholars, agree that these cases offer the best evidence yet for reincarnation. Stevenson's credentials are impeccable as well. He is a medical doctor, and has had numerous scholarly papers to his credit prior to his paranormal research. He is the former head of the Department of Psychiatry at the University of Virginia, and is now the Director of the Division of Personality Studies at the University of Virginia.

The reason that the amazing Dr. Stevenson is not better known in terms of his revolutionary research is simply that he publishes only for the academic and scientific community, and his writing, which is densely packed with research details and academic argument, is difficult for the average lay reader to follow. As well, he intentionally shuns the popular media to prevent reporters from sensationalizing his research, he refuses to appear on television or radio, and magazine interviews are rarely granted. But that doesn't prevent those interested in his work from calling attention to his amazing and vitally important discoveries. It is widely accepted that his cases are the key to widespread acceptance of reincarnation in the West, and if more people knew about these scientifically documented cases of children's past lives, they might be more likely to listen when their own young children begin to speak of "when I died before..."

Below is an excerpt from "A Matter of Life & Death," an article that appeared in the *Washington Post Magazine* in August, 1999. It was adapted from Tom Schroder's book, *Old Souls: The Scientific Evidence for Past Lives:*

It is late, nearly lightless. Smoke from a million dung fires hangs in the headlights as the Maruti microbus bangs along the narrow, cratered hardpack that passes for a paved road in the Indian outback. We are still hours away from the hotel and the possibility that we will never get there looms on as large as the absurdly overloaded truck hurtling toward us dead in the middle of the road. Using every inch of the rutted dirt shoulder, we barely escape. I can feel the truck vibrate through the thin tin of the Maruti, smell death in the exhaust pumping from the truck's tailpipe, passing at eye level. And even in escape, there is no relief: We bounce back onto the roads pitted surface and immediately overtake a wooden cart moving at the lumbering gait of a yoked oxen. It is our driver, leaning on his horn, swerves around the caret and into a blind curve that I can only pray is not already occupied by a bus loaded to the dented metal ceiling with humans and farm animals. I try not to think about the glass and metal that separates the front seat from whatever we might plow into, or the article I read that said fatal accidents are 40 times more likely on Indian roads than on American Highways. I try not to think about dying 10,000 miles from home, about never seeing my wife and children again. I try not to think about the absolute darkness. But even without my bubble of fear, I am aware of the irony. Sitting in the back seat, apparently unconcerned about the mud-splattered torpedoes racing toward us is a tall, stoop-shouldered white-haired man, nearly 80, who insists he has compiled enough solid, empirical evidence to prove that physical death is not necessarily the end of me, or anyone else. His name is Ian Stevenson, and he is a physician and psychiatrist at the University of Virginia. He has been braving roads like this for almost 37 years to bring back reports of young children who speak of remembering previous lives, providing detailed and accurate information about people who died before they were born-people they say they once were. While I struggle with my fear of dying, he is wrestling with his own fear of annihilation: that his life's work will end all but ignored by his peers.

"Why," he asks for the third time since night has fallen, "do mainstream scientists refuse to accept the evidence we have for reincarnation?" On this day, and for the past six months, Stevenson has allowed me to accompany him on two extensive field trips, first to Beirut and now to India. At first he responded to my endless questions, and even allowed me to participate in the interviews that are at the heart of his research. He evidence he is referring to does not come from fashionable new-age sources, past-life readings or hypnotic regressions. It is homely and specific: A boy remembers being a 25-year-old mechanic, thrown to his death from a speeding car on a beach road. He recalls the name of the driver, the exact location of the crash, the names of the mechanic's sisters and parents and cousins, and the people he hunted with. A girl remembers being a teenager named Sheila who was killed while crossing the road. She names the town Sheila lived in, plus Sheila's siblings and parents. When Sheila's family hears of the little girl's stories, they visit with her—in front of witnesses who say the girl recognized them by name and relationship without prompting.

From the time he learns to talk, a boy in Virginia named Joseph calls his mother by her name and calls his grandmother Mom. As he grows, Joseph begins recalling obscure events from the life of his Uncle David, a boy, who died in a accident 20 years before Joseph was born—and who has rarely been mentioned because of the family's abiding grief. It goes on and on. In scores of cases around the world, multiple witnesses confirm that children have spontaneously supplied names of towns and relatives, occupations and relationships, attitudes and emotions that pinpointed a single, dead individual—often apparently unknown to their present families.

Trying to make sense of these cases is what has involved Stevenson for almost 40 years. It is what we have been doing in Lebanon and India: examining records, interviewing witnesses and measuring the results against possible alternative explanations. And it is only now dawning won me, as we careen down a deathtrap of a rutted Indian highway that I have no easy explanations for what I've seen, and no sure answer for the question the man in the back is asking.

If Stevenson is largely ignored by his mainstream peers, in some circles he is a scientific legend. His dogged collection of cases, closing in on 3,000 now, his meticulous documentation and cross-checking, his prodigious and scholarly publication have made him a hero to many people who would like respectable reasons to distrust the radical materialism of Western science. For his own part, Stevenson has reached this conclusion:

"I think a rational person, if he wants, can believe in reincarnation on the basis of evidence."

When I first came across mention of his work, in 1989, in a footnote to an article on hypnotic regression, I wondered if he might be the kind of wacko who also had a drawer full of fragments of the True Cross or a radio that communicated with a race of blood-red dwarves on the fifth moon of Jupiter. But reading further, I found that this was clearly not the case. A 1975 article in no less than the *Journal of the American Medical Association* said Stevenson had collected cases in which 'the evidence is difficult to explain on any other grounds' beside reincarnation. The article cited a book in which Stevenson had compiled in his field studies, *Twenty Cases Suggestive of Reincarnation*. I visited a couple of bookstores and found nothing by Stevenson. The public library listed several volumes by him but could locate only *Twenty Cases*.

The prose reminded me of some of the eye-crossing anthropology texts I'd read in college, but it was worth the read…the cases were compelling, even astonishing. Each had distinct particulars, each hinted at narrative enough for a novel, but all of them shared some essential aspects; a young child was said to have spontaneously asserted another identity, recounting details of memory and knowledge that appeared to conform to someone else's life.

*Twenty Cases* and a bookshelf of similar volumes Stevenson has produced are stuffed with elaborate examinations in which he sought to determine if the things these children said and the ways they behaved could be explained in any normal' way. His methods are those of the social scientist, the detective, and the investigative reporter. He methodically tracked down and interviewed firsthand witnesses to statements a child made, especially those uttered before any contact had been made with the friends or family of the deceased (in Stevenson's terminology, the previous "personality.") He cross-examined the witnesses, noted possible motivations for bias toward or against, and meticulously charted confirmations.

Before I actually met Stevenson, the only insight I had into him personally came from a reprint of a lecture he had given at Southeastern Louisiana University in 1989, in which he explained how he progressed from analyzing rat livers in a medical lab to interviewing children who claim to remember previous lives. His remarks read like something from the 19th century, a time when scientists could also be writers, historians and philosophers, when they weren't afraid to think aloud and puzzle over something imponderable. But I was also intrigued by a subtle underlying tone of bitterness, or at least hurt and puzzlement, apparent in the text. Stevenson clearly felt that his life's work had been scorned, or merely ignored, by those mainstream scientists he considered his peers. He didn't even wait for the second paragraph to say, "For me, everything now believed by scientists is open to question, and I am always dismayed to find that many scientists accept current knowledge as forever fixed." In his darker moments, Stevenson felt like an outcast, a heretic damned for his affronts to the scientific orthodoxy.

I first met Stevenson in January 1997, at his office on the University of Virginia campus. It was in an ancient two-story frame house sandwiched between an apartment building and a high rise parking garage. A plaque on the exterior read **Division of Personality Studies**. When I was shown into Stevenson's office, we sat in facing armchairs. He spoke formally and thoughtfully. There was a sense of the past in the house, in his dress and manner and the way we were sitting there like gentlemen taking an after-dinner brandy. In that conversation, and in subsequent ones, his seriousness of purpose was constant. He was reserved, but as I got to know him in the months that followed, I found him quite willing to consider any questions, even pointed ones about his motives and background. Over dinner in a Beirut hotel, he explained what had diverted him from a successful career in conventional medical research:

"What happened was that as I was a very extensive reader, I began to find books here and there, and in newspapers and magazines, reports of what were usually individual cases of reincarnation memories. In the end I found 44 cases. The thing that came out when you got them all together was that they predominantly featured young children, ages 2 to 5, who spoke of previous life memories for a brief time until they were about 8. But you had to get them all together before that was obvious. Many were little more than journalistic anecdotes, but some were considerably more serious.

Numbers count in science, and these 44 cases, when you put them together, it just seemed inescapable to me that there must be something there. I couldn't see how they could all be faked. Or they could all be a deception. My conclusion was that this might be a promising line of investigation if more cases could be found and studied earlier and more carefully. I don't think it occurred to me that I might be the one to carry out the investigations."

After Stevenson published a paper on his survey of the literature in 1960, he began to hear reports of similar claims in India, and received invitations to investigate.

As Ralph Waldo Emerson so accurately described it, "We wake and find ourselves on a stair. There are other stairs below us which we seem to have ascended; there are stairs above us, many a one, which go upward and out of sight."

What follows are a few examples of regression sessions I have executed. The names of my clients have been altered to protect their privacy:

## PAST LIFE REGRESSION ONE

Sarah is a woman with prominent spiritual evidence who appears to have reached a time of "Soul Searching." She is extraordinarily attractive; a physical attribute, I believe, she has borne for many lifetimes. A double-edged sword, her beauty has both helped and hindered her former incarnations. She also boasts an extremely strong sense of "self," another trait capable of aiding or, possibly blocking, her spiritual growth, although I got the impression she employs this trait in an extremely positive manner, at least in this lifetime, a trait that will surely benefit her in the future. There appears to be a relationship with another in which she feels extremely "uncomfortable" and though I am convinced this bond is "destiny related," I found little evidence during her regression of any former connections between them. The following is an account of Sarah's regression once under hypnosis:

> I am alone, walking across a bridge. The day is cloudy. I stop and look into the water. It is gray and calm. I notice my hands are numb. I'm wearing a yellow garment and have no shoes on. I have no friends. It is getting very dark. My hands are very soft. I see lots of grass. There is my house—it is brick and has one story. I have a good feeling about my house. I live alone and look after this house and my dog. I have no Aunts or Uncles. I go to school and like it very much. I want

to have a job. I do all right at school and have a good friend named Sheila. I am sixteen years old. There are many noises around me. Many other ladies chatting and looking outside the window. They all wear veils. I like it here very much. It is a harem. I am fifteen years old and very, very pretty. I am the favorite. I think the year is 1920.

As I took her through the next lifetime it was interesting to note that Sarah preferred to disassociate herself from the "little girl," describing her as "someone else" when indeed she is describing herself in another lifetime.

I see a little girl about three or four years old. She is very, very happy. She never wants to get married, if she does, she will miss out on all the attention. It is evening. The sky is pink and blue. I look out and see beautiful healthy trees around me. I can see people getting down from the tree house. There must have been a celebration of some kind, perhaps a wedding. They are all walking down the road. I am alone now and in the tree house.

I am content to be alone. I am wearing a white garment and am twenty years of age. I see something outside. A dark figure moving about. An old heavy guy is climbing, coming to get me. He is very heavy. He attacks me and rapes me. I notice how heavy he is. When he is finished he just laughs and laughs. He then leaves me alone. I am very sad. I will never marry.

Since Sarah's past lives were revealed to her in an extremely sporadic and scattered manner, it was difficult to establish exactly what part of her present relationship tied in with her past lives. There was, however, a common thread running through the few incarnations she touched upon. It appeared she preferred to be alone most of the time and was extremely self-sufficient. This, coupled with the fact that she relished the attention her beauty bought her, lends to a paradoxical nature, a trait most evident in her present lifetime, particularly in terms of her inability to end a relationship she feels has run its course.

It is extremely rare to identify, in the course of just one regression session, answers to many of the queries that arise in the present incarnation. Should Sarah continue to pursue the regression therapy, perhaps the answer will be revealed to her...then again, perhaps not. That which is revealed to us is exactly what is supposed to be revealed. Nothing more, nothing less.

## PAST LIFE REGRESSION TWO

Teresa is, what I would term, a soul of considerable age. Since the age of eight (possibly before) she has perceived powerful feelings of déjà vu. An intelligent and articulate woman, her spirituality is very much in evidence. Placing far less importance on the material than on the substance of "spirit" she is basically (in her words) "a happy and contented person." There are, however, periods of depression that, according to Teresa, "nothing or no one can bring me out of."

Having recently lost a considerable amount of money, coupled with the end of an "arranged" marriage (events that could seriously depress almost anyone), Teresa is adamant in her belief that everything is exactly as it should be (an adage that I personally, strongly adhere to). The fact that Teresa is curious as to whether or not she is paying off old karmic debts or creating new ones is neither here nor there. Teresa had been suffering from periodic bouts of depression prior to the aforementioned events.

> The year is 1844 and I am twenty years old...I am at a fair in the village. There are lots of people here, dancing and laughing. I can hear the music and I feel good. I am wearing a yellow outfit and I am dancing too. There is a man there...a stranger to the village. He is wearing white. I feel like I have

known him before. There is an attraction on my part. I hope to see him again. I think of him off and on, but I am married. I hardly know my husband as he lives in a different house. There are no children. I am unhappy and want to leave this village just to get away…to be someplace different. I spend my time gardening and do some sewing. My husband comes to this house once in awhile to bring me money. We have sex when he wants to. My parents live in another village.

(I bring her 30 years forward to the age of 50)

I'm still in the same house. My husband died from too much drink. I don't drink; he wanted me to, and I tried it once but didn't like it. The only person I talk to is the maid. She understands my loneliness…she knows how I feel inside…I don't even have to tell her. She understands. She has to leave me and evacuate with all the others as she has a family. I don't know why everyone in the village is gone…I don't know why they had to leave. I don't think it was because of sickness, but I am all alone. I still think of the stranger in white…he came back to the village several times. I believe he was a cousin of my husband. He looked at me with only respect.

(I bring her 25 years forward to the age of 75)

I am in a small, very old house. It is so old it is dirty. I see a white vase with blue stripes and yellow flowers in this place. I am very unhappy. It seems everyone in the village has left, I don't know why, but they had to leave the village. I was left behind…maybe I was too old to go.

I am walking toward a mountain…I am looking for something or someone, I don't know what. On the way, I pass a white house. It belonged to the richest man in the village. He and his family had to leave with the others. I don't go inside. I just look in the window. I didn't leave with the others because I was waiting for the man in white to come back but he didn't. I waited for him to return.

(At this point Teresa goes forward, but is unable to tell me how old she is)

I am standing outside. I don't recognize the village. I don't know what I'm doing here. There are lots of plants and a building with glass...windows, I think. My feet are bare. No, there is what looks like...leather tied on them. I am a very old woman...very old. I have no one and am very lonely. It seems I am waiting or searching for something but I don't know where I am.

I know now! The building with glass is a hospital. There is nothing wrong with me physically, but I have some kind of mental illness. I am very confused and depressed. I think I am still waiting for something or someone; I don't know. I can't think straight, and I've lost the ability to talk. I think of the man in white and that makes me happy. I am only happy when I think of him. The name *Sanjay* comes to my mind when I think of him. I am treated well at the hospital, but I can't talk to anyone. I have been here a very long time. I have no fear of death. I never had any children. I am lonely and depressed.

There was no recall as to whether or Teresa died in hospital, however, circumstances were such that it was highly probable. The acute sense of depression she experienced throughout most of that particular lifetime could account for her periodic bouts of depression in this lifetime.

# TERESA'S SECOND REGRESSION SESSION

"I am thirty-one years old. I'm married and content. My husband, Sanjay, is studying for his degree in medicine."

(Teresa jumps ahead to sometime in the future)

"We have two children now...a boy and a girl. We live in another town and Sanjay has his own practice. There is very little money, but we are at peace."

In this lifetime, Teresa dies before her husband. In her words:

"I died from a 'sudden and unexpected death'...a shock...not painful."

She recalls the complete sense of acceptance she felt immediately following the death experience. I was about to guide Teresa back when she suddenly commented:

"I am on the floor. I don't know why I'm here."

I didn't expect Teresa's immediate leap into a third life, but this type of occurrence is not unusual during life-regression therapy. She began to describe the floor she was standing on as "cement or concrete."

"My father is on the bed...lying there, and my mother just walked in the door. She is crying. I am about eight months old. My mother is mentally depressed."

At this point Teresa began to cry. I take her forward to the age of 10.

"I feel responsible for my mother because she is still depressed. I feel responsible because she has to raise my younger brother and me by herself. My father died a few years ago."

# SIX

## Auras

Ever since I can remember I've had the ability to see people's auras, and it wasn't long before I was able to discern how the various colors of these individuals related to their personality and character. For example, I could always tell if someone was lying to me. Auras are generally visible at a time when the onlooker is in a state of complete relaxation such as driving, listening to soothing music, et cetera.

To cite a personal example, I was attending a piano concert at Massey Hall in Toronto with a friend of mine a few years ago when my eyes were drawn to the most beautiful auras I'd ever seen emanating from a woman seated a few rows ahead of us. My friend, a rather reserved individual, kept asking me to be quiet as I raved to her about the woman's exquisite aura. Following the concert, she had to literally hold me back from approaching the woman in the lobby of the theatre as I wanted to introduce myself and applaud her exquisite aura. Our auras react to everyone we come in contact as our energies are intermingling. Therefore, if the frequencies of our auras are similar we feel comfortable, if not, we feel uncomfortable. Or perhaps there is an unexplained dislike of the other individual, or worse still, we feel completely drained as many people will, albeit unknowingly, sap our energy. It is important to maintain a strong aura and this can be accomplished by eliminating negative habits such as alcohol, stress, poor diet, and replace them with soothing music, fresh air, sunshine and meditation.

The Webster's New World Dictionary describes the "aura" as *an invisible emanation or vapor.* It's been described as a colored outline emanating from every living thing such a humans, plants, animals and trees. A colored field of energy surrounds us, and every color depicts a particular characteristic of the possessor. As well, our auras react to everyone we come in contact with so if our auras are similar to another individual we feel comfortable, if not, we may feel ill at ease. The main part of the color and energy in the aura is provided and activated by the action of the chakras. (The body has spinning energy centers that resemble spinning wheels and are called chakras.) As with all things in our reality, they are linked to sound, light and color. To heal is to bring the chakras into alignment and balance. The color of an individual's aura reveals where their awareness is centered, be it in the mental, physical, intellectual or spiritual realm. An imbalance between these two realms combined with the action of the chakras causes the aura to fluctuate, the two main fluctuations being the shape and color. The majority of the color changes in one's aura result from changes within and all colors are apt to intensify or fade according to the individual's mood, be it emotional, physical or mental state. Above all, the spiritual state plays an enormous part in altering the size and shape of the aura.

# AURA COLORS AND WHAT THEY SIGNIFY

**Purple:**                                 Indicates intense spirituality.

**Blue:**                                     Indicates balance and relaxation. Individuals who have blue as a strong color in their aura are life sustainers and lead a balanced existence. Their nervous system is completely relaxed and they are natural survivors. They are cool, calm, caring, loving and love to assist others, intuitive and sensitive. Oddly enough, when an individual with a blue aura is sending or receiving any information telepathically, the regular blue aura changes to an electric blue. Michel Desmarquet, author of *Thiaoouba Prophesy* frequently glows with the electric blue during his discourses and lectures, particularly when he is answering questions from the audience.

**Soft Blue:**                       Indicates peacefulness, truthfulness, communication and intuition.

**Bright Royal Blue:**      Indicates a highly spiritual nature, generosity and clairvoyance.

**Dark or Muddy Blue:**    Indicates a fear of self-expression, fear of being truthful and fear of the future.

**Indigo:**                            Relates to the third eye, visual and pituitary gland. Indicates sensitivity and very deep feelings.

**Turquoise:**                    Relates to the immune system and is an indication of an individual who is dynamic, highly energized and a strong influence on others. Outstanding organizers, they are capable of doing a number of things, simultaneously, feeling bored and restless when having to concentrate on just one thing. Individuals with turquoise auras make excellent bosses as they carefully explain their goals rather than demanding them. Those with a turquoise aura are known to be sensitive, compassionate and often become therapists or healers.

**Green:** Indicates a natural healing ability, a gift belonging to all natural healers are much centered on love. The stronger the green aura, the better the healer. They also love gardening and more often than not have a "green thumb"—anything grows for them. Just being in the presence of an individual with a green aura is extremely peaceful, almost restful experience. It also relates to the heart and lungs and is representative of love of nature, animals and fellow man.

**Green (Dark or Muddy):** Indicates jealousy, resentment, insecurity, low self-esteem, lack of understanding, and sensitive to perceived criticism.

**Yellow:** A yellow aura indicates a sense of joy and freedom. Individuals with yellow auras are extremely generous and free from attachments to earthly things. If the aura is high above the head and "halo shaped" it is a sign of one who is a spiritual teacher. It is a given that one should never accept spiritual advice or teachings from anyone who doesn't have a yellow halo. Both Christ and Buddha's yellow halos extended to their arms and it is a rarity in this day and age to find an individual whose yellow aura/halo is any larger than one inch. It is the color of awakening, intelligence, inspiration and optimism.

**Light or Pale Yellow:** Indicates an emerging spiritual and psychic Awareness.

**Yellow-Green:** Creative with heart—communicative.

**Orange:** An orange aura indicates a sign of power and ability (or desire) to control others. Often, when the orange is at its strongest; it contributes to a yellow halo, which in turn becomes gold, an indication of a powerful spiritual teacher. It also relates to reproductive organs and emotions. It is the color of vitality, vigor, good health and excitement and indicates a great deal of energy and stamina and creativity as well as an individual who is productive, courageous, and adventurous and has an outgoing social nature.

**Orange Yellow:** Is a sign of an intelligent, detail-oriented, scientific perfectionist.

**Orange Red:** Shows confidence and creative power.

| | |
|---|---|
| **Red:** | A red aura indicates materialistic thoughts and relates to the physical body, heart and circulation. A predominantly red aura is an indication of a materialistic individual. The densest color, it creates the most friction. Also indicates money worries, obsessions, anger, unforgiveness, anxiety and nervousness. |
| **Deep Red:** | Indicates a realistic, survivalist and well-grounded individual. |
| **Muddied Red:** | Indicates anger (repelling). |
| **Clear Red:** | Passionate, compassionate, energetic and competitive. |
| **Pink:** | Signifies love (in a spiritual sense). To obtain a clear pink, you have to mix the purple (the highest frequency we perceive) with red (the lowest frequency). A pink aura indicates that the individual has achieved a perfect balance between spiritual awareness and the material existence. The most advanced individuals have not only a yellow halo around the head (a permanent strong point in the aura) but also a large pink aura extending further away. The pink color in the aura is extremely rare on earth and appears only as a temporary thought, never as a strong point in the aura. |
| **Pink (Bright and Light):** | Indicates a loving, tender, compassionate, sensitive, sensual, artistic and |

pure individual. It can also indicate clairaudience.

**Dark and Murky Pink:** Indicates immaturity and/or dishonest nature.

**Lavender:** Denotes great imagination... a visionary... daydreamer.

**Violet:** The most intuitive color in terms of auras; as well as being the most sensitive and wisest in that it reveals true psychic power of attunement with self. It is extremely intuitive, idealistic and artistic.

**Brown:** A brown aura indicates a negating, unsettling and materialistic individual as well as a "holding on" to energy that needs to be released. Someone who takes freely, but rarely gives is likely to have a brown discoloration of congested energies.

**Gray:** A gray aura indicates dark and depressing thoughts, unclear intentions and the presence of a dark side of personality.

**Dark Muddy Gray:** Indicates that a residue of fear is accumulating in the body with a potential for health problems, particularly if the gray clusters are seen in specific areas of the body.

**Black:** A black aura tends to draw or pull energy into it and in so doing, transforms it. It captures light and consumes it. Generally indicates a long-term unforgiveness toward others or another.

**White:**     A white aura is a pure state of light often representing a new, not yet designated energy in the aura. Spiritual, etheric and non-physical qualities, transcendent, higher dimensions, purity and truth as well as angelic qualities. White sparkles or flashes of white light indicate the angels are nearby and also indicate that a woman is pregnant or will be soon.

**Silver:**     The color of abundance, both spiritual as well as physical. A great deal of silver reflects a great deal of money and/or an awakening of the cosmic mind.

**Bright Metallic Silver:**     Indicates that the individual is receptive to new ideas and is extremely intuitive and nurturing.

**Gold:**     Indicates enlightenment and divine protection. When seen within the aura, it indicates the individual is guided by their highest good. It is divine guidance. Also indicates an individual who is intuitive, knowledgeable and wise (with a great deal of inner wisdom) and spirituality as well.

**Earth Aura Colors:**     Soil, wood, mineral, plant. These colors display a love of the earth, of being grounded and is seen in those who live and work on the outdoors… construction, farming, etc. These colors are important and are a good sign.

**Rainbows:** Rainbow-colored stripes, protruding like sunbeams from the hand; head or body indicates an individual who is in the first incarnation on earth. It also represents someone who is a Reiki healer.

**Pastels:** A pastel aura is an indication of sensitivity and a powerful need for security. A sensitive blend of light and color, more so than basic colors. Shows sensitivity and need for serenity.

## AURA COLOR CHANGES

As the colors of our aura breathe, expand and contract, the various colors therein begin to dance. If an individual is in good health, the colors are bright, pure and quite strong and dense. Happiness creates a slightly shiny, sparkling effect and feelings of love completely cover the aura with the colors of violet and pink. If an individual is feeling sad, the low energy level causes the aura colors to become dimmer, sometimes to the point of complete dullness. It stands to reason I suppose that "dreamy" individuals have rather faint auras as they are less physically grounded, resulting in less coloring.

The two most common discolorations of the aura are brown and gray. They are results of "energy in" not equal to "energy out." A gray aura suggests the creation of an obstruction to some type of energy input. Examples would be: fear of emotional involvement (emotional level); unwillingness to accept another's ideas (mental level); or lack of desire for food (metabolic or physical level).

# AURA SHAPE CHANGES

Not surprisingly "shock" is the most likely cause of shape changes to the aura. It can either shift the aura from the head and heart, leaving both unprotected. This incident causes your physical sensations to separate from your spirit, and if the shock is severe enough to shift the aura away from the heart area, your emotions will no longer feel connected to your body. The individual will feel as though they are having a nervous breakdown and will likely experience a fainting spell. A less severe shock (such as witnessing an accident) generally regularizes in about twenty-four hours, but during that time, the individual may feel vulnerable, insecure, and unable to accept any form of responsibility. There is a definite lack of connection between the personality and mental activities. On the other hand, a mild shock (falling or cutting oneself) may shift the aura from the head just momentarily. Taking a deep breath will shift the protective aura back into place.

It should come as no surprise that negative emotions can also alter the shape of the aura. Jealousy and hate produce a jagged edge to the auric layers, thereby weakening the structure and undermining your protection. Even the food we eat has a definite impact on the quality of our aura colors. Highly processed foods, particularly foods that are packaged, sealed and stored, lack energy and produce a correspondingly thin aura. Eating too much meat causes the aura to become considerably dimmer as well.

The change in your consciousness is also reflected in your aura. For example, the normal, beta pulse rate (during normal human activity it's 21 cycles per second) produces the typical multi-colored aura, but as your rate slows to alpha (13 cycles per second), the aura shows a blue overlay. At seta (8 cycles per second), the blue gives way to gold, and if the delta state is reached (5 cycles per second), the aura is almost white, lightly tinged with magenta. In effect, you are moving through all the levels of consciousness of the evolutionary process.

The ability to see auras was, at one time, considered to be a talent possessed strictly by witches or psychics; however, (as has happened in the area of telepathy) it has now been proven to be as much a natural law as walking and talking. This has been proven by the discovery, in 1939, of Kirlian photography, developed by Semyon and Valentina Kirlian from Krasnadar in the Soviet Union. They produced photographs of light flares surrounding people, plants and various inanimate objects. Called "bioluminescence," these flares of light are varied in color and degrees of intensity and provide us with pictures of the electromagnetic force fields emanating from their subjects—in other words, "the auras" of their subjects. It has become a serious area of study in many parts of the world and is used, in the Soviet Union, to aid medical diagnosis.

# SEVEN

## Life Before Birth

### PRENATAL MEMORIES

Psychology traditionally placed the beginnings of memory at about age three as very few individuals have conscious recall of events prior to that age; however, an accumulating amount of scientific research demonstrates that the memory is active from as early as the prenatal stage. A number of children spontaneously recall birth experiences, but are unable to voice them until they learn to talk. They are, however, able to express their memories non-verbally by pointing to body locations, acting out scenes in pantomime, drawing pictures and even providing authentic sound effects (like suction devices) used at birth.

Recent research into this phenomenon has been made possible by direct ultrasound observations of fetal behavior. For example, twins can be observed developing certain habits and gestures at twenty weeks gestational age that persist into their postnatal years. In one case, a brother and sister were observed playing cheek-to-cheek on either side of the dividing membrane and at one year of age, their favorite game was to take positions on opposite sides of a curtain, and laugh as they touched each other and played through the curtain.

Parents interested in prenatal communication have taught their unborn children the "Kick Game." When they feel the babies kick, the parents touch the abdomen and say, "Kick, baby, kick!" When the baby kicks, they move to a different location and repeat the invitation. The babies soon oblige by kicking anywhere on cue. In a famous experiment by Anthony DeCasper and colleagues at the University of North Carolina, pregnant women read the Dr. Seuss story, *The Cat In the Hat,* at regular intervals before birth. At birth, the babies were hooked up to recordings that they could select by sucking on a non-nutritive nipple. After a few trials, babies cleverly sucked at whatever speed was necessary to obtain their mother's voice reading *The Cat in the Hat.* Similarly, in utero, musical passages repeated regularly—

such as theme music for the British soap opera, *Neighbours,* or the bassoon passage from *Peter and the Wolf* are identified and preferred immediately after birth. In a recent experiment, French mothers repeated a children's rhyme each day from week 33 to week 37 of gestation. At the end of this time (still inside the womb) the babies showed memory and learning for this particular rhyme as opposed to similar rhymes they had not heard.

Infants are learning their native language before birth. This is made possible by the development of hearing as early as 16 weeks gestational age. A mother's voice reaches the uterus with very little distortion as the sound waves pass directly through her body. Acoustic spectroscopy, which makes possible elaborately detailed portraits of sound similar to fingerprints, has documented prenatal learning of the mother tongue and by 27 weeks of gestation, the cry of a baby already contains some of the speech features, rhythms, and voice characteristics of its mother. Newborn reactions to language are based on the sounds heard in utero.

For example, French babies prefer to look at persons speaking French while Italian babies prefer to watch people speaking Italian.

Unexpected evidence for prenatal learning and memory comes from studies of taste and olfaction (sense of smell). Until recently, olfaction was thought to require air; therefore, the learning of odors was not considered possible before birth. Current evidence, however, recognizes the complex interaction of chemosensory receptors in utero. Many chemical compounds, including those from the mother's diet, pass through the placenta and reach the baby in utero while others flow in the capillaries of the nasal mucosa. By breathing and swallowing amniotic fluid, a baby becomes familiar with the mother's diet, including things like garlic. Even before post-nasal exposure to breast milk, babies already know and prefer their own mother's milk. Abrupt changes in her diet during the perinatal period can confuse babies and upset breastfeeding.

Unborn babies are able to lean their mother's emotional state as well. Experiments in Australia revealed that unborn babies were participating in the emotional upset of their mothers as they watched a disturbing 20-minute segment of a Hollywood movie. When briefly re-exposed to this film up to three months after birth, they still showed recognition of the earlier experience. Studies of a thousand babies whose mothers had experienced various degrees of depression during pregnancy themselves displayed depression at birth and in proportion to the depression scores of their mothers.

An important message of these diverse findings is that memory and learning seem to be a natural part of being human, including the first nine months in the womb and the years of infancy, defined as the time before speech. Perhaps the biggest surprise is that life in the womb is extremely active and interactive and the womb is, in fact, a classroom. Though rare, a number of individuals are able to recall an existence shortly prior to their being born into this world. The pre-birth experience (PBE) is one of the most fascinating areas of psychic-research. Not to be confused with "past-life memories" wherein one recalls their previous lives as humans on earth, sometimes recently or perhaps hundreds or even thousands of years ago, the pre-birth experience involves the memory of life in the same or similar plane of existence.

Some who claim to have had this fascinating experience recall being in a spirit world and are fully aware of earth. Often, they are able to choose their next life or communicate with their future parents. Some individuals who have had an NDE (Near-Death Experience) have reported this same experience. Research into this phenomena has identified the characteristics, traits, and types of PBE's as well as when, where, and to whom they occur. Of these individuals surveyed, 53% remembered a time before conception, and 47% after conception but before birth.

It should come as no surprise that children are the most common source of information regarding PBE's as they are spontaneous and eager to share their memories. One such incident is revealed in the book, *Coming From The Light* by Sarah Hinze:

> I was putting three-year-old Johnny to bed when he asked for a bedtime story. For the past few weeks, I had been telling him of the adventures of his great-great-grandfather: a colonizer, a soldier and a community leader. As I started another story, Johnny stopped me and said, "No, tell me of Grandpa Robert." I was surprised. This was my grandpa. I had not told stories of him, and I could not imagine where he had heard his name. He had died before I had even married. "How do you know about Grandpa Robert?" I asked. "Well, Momma," he said with reverence, "he's the one who brought me to earth."

No less compelling is this excerpt from Michael Maguire's experience:

> I can remember standing in a dark space, but unlike being in a darkened room, I could see everything around me and the blackness had dimension. There was another person standing

to my right, and like me, he was waiting to be born into the physical world. There was an older person with us who could possibly be a guide, since he stayed with us until we left and answered my questions. In front of us and approximately 30 degrees below us, we could see the Earth with the facial images of two couples. I asked who those people were whose images appeared on the Earth and he replied that they were going to be our parents. The older man conveyed to us that it was time to go. The other person standing next to me walked forward and disappeared from my sight. I was told that it was my turn and I walked forward. Suddenly, I found myself lying in a hospital nursery with other babies around me.

Author, musician and teacher, Frank Westcott, unlike the majority of individuals who have had an PBE experience, was adamant that he not be born. As Frank tells it:

I do know and remember before coming to Earth this time, not wanting to come and sitting around with others, twelve I think, with others behind them…the key twelve and others too trying to convince me to come…I saw what I would be walking into…and I wanted no part of it… and I argued and I basically was not going to come. I was a fairly evolved, respected soul of some position for lack of a better word and there was an element of choice there for me. I didn't have to come. I remember being quite happy where I was. I really liked it there. I kept listening to the others. Especially the twelve. And there were angels flying and flitting about in their way. And I remember being told by them that they would be here with me, that they would come, too. I remember asking them and re-checking with different ones and getting them to and having them state/declare that they would be here with me...for the whole way...no coming back...or sneaking back on their part...that I would not be alone... ever...in this...that they would support me....through this...always...I remember them or some entity saying that if I agreed to come this trip that it would not be necessary for me to do it again in this form....ever... This had a payoff to me... a value in my decision and agreement to come. And I remember there being a sense or feeling in me of duty, of obligation to come to help others in some way by my coming...that there was something larger in my coming than just being here...doing the life thing...and getting on with it...something that would have a positive impact on the Earth entities...and energies of entities in and around here... It was like I had some knowing, or knowledge, or something that would make it so...and also that because of my own forces and power in my entity I had the power to withstand and handle (in the end or on the journey in the silent places of the soul) the abuse, trauma etc. that I was walking into on an Earthly level for a larger purpose. I don't get this or understand it other than to say that I remember the feeling of this at that pre-birth time...I remember those around me trying to convince me to come and that after I got through all the "stuff" there would be large rewards for me...I remember these things in pre-birth as well as other world memories before coming to Earth this time in this form...so I am just sharing them with you as they are/were.

I remember being in the womb and quite liking it there, too, actually and having fun floating around in the water. Kind of liked that form. The cord got in the way sometimes, kind of got pissed off with that...but learned to keep it out of the way or float by it if I moved right...and I liked the floating freedom in there…and it was warm…and not too bad…and there was a brightness there…a funny striated kind of coloration or something… like it wasn't pure darkness…or all black in there as you would think…I remember being pissed off when the water broke…that REALLY MADE ME ANGRY…like my free ride was over…the fun in the womb was over… and quite frankly I did not want to come out. Period. End of story. I knew what I was coming out to. I gave them (earth entities) a hard time coming out. I tried to go back actually. No luck. "It's a Long Way Home" as one of my songs in the Without Shame Tour list says.

Regarding his pre-birth-experience, Frank had this to say:

I believe we all have our purposes and that in this we shall know of ourselves and that in this there is no higher learning, being, form. I believe this. I believe this is, in part, what we are here to discover. Each of us. To bring light to our essential core that our light can then brighten the world in the way of angels, in the way of angels who constantly, if we listen, whisper in our ears. Like that. I think it is like that somehow, someway…I do not know what the secret was to survival or being the person I am even though coming through such a life. When I ask myself this question the response is: "That was who I was. That is who I am" in that my essence, my essential core was and is and has always been this, the Frank you know and feel when I am with you, that this was and is so strong, so powerful that it could not be shaken or destroyed through the machinations of my parents, surrogates, and others…in the end. Perhaps there is a lesson in this for all of us, in that "who" we are in our essential innermost selves is true and full of light….and safe and still there for us no matter what life in this life has brought to us, or caused us to encounter and ultimately choose to face or not and grow from. I know I have been truly blessed on this journey this time. I know I have had protectors, and angel energies swirling about me for eons…and hugely on this trip, even though I was not always, minute-to-minute conscious of their presence. I pretty much am now. The "why" I do not know. The "reason" I do not know. Not at a level of conscious expression, anyway.

Frank had every reason to be hesitant about leaving the womb. As a child he suffered sexual abuse at the hands of numerous family members. When I asked if he wanted the general public to know of his sexual abuse, he said:

If the fact I was abused leads to anything positive… be it useful in your book, be it leading to others understanding something in their own lives and leading them through this understanding to some healing, absolutely yes. I believe when one of us heals it opens the doorway for others to heal…whether we know of them or not.

# EIGHT

## Life After Death

*"The sheer volume of evidence for survival after death is so
immense that to ignore it is like standing at the foot of
Mount Everest and insisting that you cannot see the mountain."*

*Colin Wilson - world authority on psychic phenomena.*

World-renowned scientist Dr. Robert Crookall, DSC, PhD, undertook a
systematic study of hundreds of communications from the afterlife and
in 1961 published the results in his book, *The Supreme Adventure*.

In his book, Dr. Crookall makes the following statements about
life after death:

1.  All humans survive physical death, irrespective of their beliefs.

2.  At the point of death we take our mind with all its experiences, our
    character and our etheric (spirit) body—which is a duplicate of the

earth body. It comes out of the earth body on the point of death and is connected to the earth body by a silver chord. Death occurs when the silver cord is severed from the physical body. Silver Birch, a High Intelligence from the afterlife who has transmitted more than nine books, informs us that in the afterlife the etheric body and our surroundings will be just as solid as our world seems to us now.

3. Immediately after physical death many may feel an urge to lift themselves upwards.

4. The state of mind at the point of death is crucial. Some pass over consciously and are fully aware of the loved ones who come to welcome the new arrival; others are unconscious and are taken to a special place of rest like a hospital or rest home. Anyone who has been sick for some time will need time to readjust his or her mental picture.

5. Some people at the point of death find it easy to get out of the dead physical body. With others, helpers need to actively assist in the transition. Some very materialistic people will have a very heavy duplicate body and it will be more difficult for them to separate from their dead physical body.

6. A WARNING: Some hallucinogenic drugs have the potency to lift the duplicate out of the physical body. Seen by entities from the afterlife, drug takers…have pathetic looks as if they had no soul…they are vacant behind the eyes. When out of the body other lower entities try to enter the drug-taker's body—then you have "possession."

7. There is no such thing as heaven "up in the sky" or hell "down below"—the location of the afterlife does not change from the earth plane—different spheres interpenetrate—from the highest vibrations to the lowest.

8. Those with dogmatic, unalterable fixed ideas about what to ex-

pect immediately after death are likely to experience serious problems.

9. Atheists, agnostics and others may not be encumbered from passing on to the higher spheres—what they did in their lifetime and the motivation for what they did will be important not what they believed in.

10. Love, unconditional love, is the most powerful force known in the universe.

11. Unconditional love is the irretrievable link with our loved ones in the afterlife.

12. Decent folk are met by their loved ones—soul mates are reunited. Higher Intelligences inform us that in the afterlife our appearance can regress to our best age—for most people from the early-mid twenties.

13. Loved ones from the afterlife, recently arrived and others, do have the power to visit loved ones still living on earth.

14. Recently arrived loved ones, usually within three months of transition, are permitted to transmit visually—by way of dreams or by apparition and other means—evidence that they are still alive.

15. The kind of life to be lived in the afterlife—beauty, peace, light and love that awaits decent folk is unimaginable.

16. One can still learn spiritual lessons in the afterlife and progress to higher even more beautiful spheres.

17. Once you enter the afterlife, you will experience a feeling of enormous lightness.

18. Any physical disabilities people had on earth will disappear—for decent folk there will be no such thing as deformity, sickness, blindness or any other thing which adversely affected them on earth.

19. The mind has enormous power in the afterlife. It can create matter

there and can cause the body to travel at the speed of thought, eg: You imagine you are at any place in the world and you are there instantly.

20. Those who were consistently evil are either left alone or are met by those others of the same very low vibrations, with the same very low spirituality to be attracted to the darker lower spheres.

21. Some people on earth have a much better transition to the afterlife than others—the more knowledge we have about the afterlife, the easier the transition.

22. Some people get stuck "between the two worlds." Because they still feel themselves solid, they do not accept that they have actually died. Many get into mental confusion and could get lost for decades and for much longer.

23. Those who on earth were deeply caught in habits and vices—tobacco, alcohol, gambling, drugs or overindulgence in sex can get caught on the astral level and will not progress until they are prepared to give up these habits.

24. Energy—a universal law—positive or negative—is a "boomerang." When you send out good energy towards someone that good energy is returned sooner or later. If you send out negative energy by unfairly being dishonest against someone, or by cheating or lying or harassing or discrediting or causing harm to someone—that kind of negative energy will inevitably return to you.

25. "You will reap what you sow" is the recognized universal spiritual law. Karma means you will not get away with it. All negative deeds against others have to be experienced for the purpose of "continuous spiritual refinement."

26. Every thought, every word and deed is recorded…you will be held accountable.

27. In the higher spheres you will be able to recall and see any event

in any period of your existence three dimensionally.

28. Abuse of power and systematic harassment of others are two of the most karmic actions. Horrific karma awaits those whose task it was to protect society but themselves willfully abused their power, indulged in willful transgressions and caused harm and injury to others.

29. You will NOT be excused for your evil behavior by claiming that you were just obeying orders.

30. Cruelty—mental or physical against humans or animals—is highly karmic and is never justified.

31. It is guaranteed that those who consistently abuse and harass others will have to face their victims, in the afterlife before severest retribution.

32. After the severest retribution of those who intentionally harassed and deliberately violated other peoples' rights, the transgressors will have to apologize and seek forgiveness by the victims before they are allowed to make any progress.

33. Hell for eternity and eternal damnation were invented by men to manipulate the hearts and the minds of the unaware—they do NOT exist. Whilst there ARE lower spheres in the afterlife which are particularly dark, unpleasant and even horrific—some call them "hell"—ending up there is NOT for eternity. The universal Law of Progress ensures that at some time in the future those with lower vibrations will eventually, even if it takes eons of time—centuries even thousands of years—obtain higher vibrations and graduate to the higher spheres.

34. No one judges you or condemns you to the lower spheres. You condemn yourself to the lower horrific spheres ("hell") by the low vibrations (low spirituality) you acquired during life on earth.

35. Deathbed conversion? We have been and we are repeatedly being

informed by Higher Sources that immediately after we die our vibrations do not change— not even if one repents shortly before death. We take with us the accumulated vibrations (spirituality) we gained or lost during our whole lifetime on earth. Baptism and repentance is absolutely meaningless as a way of getting "a better deal" immediately after death.

36. If you helped just one person to attain the true knowledge you would have justified your existence on earth. —*Silver Birch*.

37. Preventing others from accessing true knowledge is highly karmic.

38. No one on earth or elsewhere can hurt you spiritually.

39. People on earth are not all born spiritually equal.

40. Selfishness is one of the greatest transgressions against spirituality and is highly karmic.

41. Not everybody has to "reincarnate."

42. You do not come into this world to have a dream run—without pain, suffering, without problems. The more varied your experience, the more learning from many mistakes, the more valuable your lifetime.

43. Many of you will be cheated, maligned, unfairly harassed…but justice will be done…not in your world maybe but certainly in the world to come.

44. The universal laws operate whether or not you are aware of them.

45. Whenever there is an inconsistency between science and a belief system such as religion, traditional belief or skepticism, science inevitably prevails.

46. Being religious does not necessarily mean being spiritual.

47. Not participating in religious rituals eg. baptism, confessions and non-belief in creeds and dogmas does not encumber anyone from

attaining higher spiritually and the higher afterlife spheres.

48. In the afterlife communicating is done by telepathy.

49. Communicating from and to the earth plane with those in the afterlife can be (and is being) done by telepathy.

50. There are inherent dangers communicating with entities from the afterlife.

51. Those from the afterlife can read our minds and can put thoughts and ideas into our minds. Lower, mischievous entities can put negative thoughts and ideas and the positive more enlightened entities assist us with positive thoughts and ideas. A great deal is left to the exercise of free will.

52. We are at liberty to call the powerful protectors from the afterlife to assist us in coping with our everyday problems but they will not make decisions for us.

53. Materialists and others spend too much time worrying about their last ten or twenty years on earth and do not spend a tiny fraction of their time thinking what's going to happen to them in the next ten, twenty thousand years, fifty thousand years and much, very much longer.

54. What will happen to a person who suicides will depend on a number of things. Motivation is always very important. For example, there will be a big difference if one commits suicide because of inevitable death and one who suicides to avoid responsibilities. Those who take their own lives to avoid problems and responsibilities are likely to increase their problems and responsibilities in the afterlife.

55. There are different levels of spheres in the afterlife—from the lowest vibrations to the highest. On physical death we go to the sphere, which can accommodate the vibrations we accumulated throughout our life on earth. Simplistically put, most decent folk are likely

to go to the "third" sphere—some people call the summerland. The higher the vibrations, the better the conditions—which will take us to the higher spheres. We are informed that the higher spheres are too beautiful to even imagine. For those with very, very low vibrations, very serious problems do exist.

56. Consistent with the Law of Progress, eventually, even if it takes eons of time, all will progress to the higher spheres.

57. Like attracts like in the afterlife. Unlike on the earth plane, those with lower vibrations cannot mix freely with those in the higher spheres.

58. There truly is a war between the Forces of the Light and the Forces of Darkness. Those who continuously disseminate darkness: ignorance, false and pernicious propaganda, hatred, harassment of others, abuse of power, lying, cheating, dominance to exploit and other negative energy will attract—and are very likely to become part of the Forces of Darkness. Those others spreading and working towards greater understanding, knowledge, peace, love, light, harmony and other positive energy will attract and become part of the Forces of the Light.

59. Self-responsibility—ultimately, you yourself are responsible for all acts and omissions during your time on the earth plane.

## WHAT EXACTLY IS HELL?

What exactly is Hell? Are the stories we've all heard about this horrifying place fact or fantasy? Research and information transmitted from the afterlife from numerous countries around the world has an steadfast consistency: the afterlife consists of "spheres"—those from with the lowest "vibrations"—the worst, to the highest, the best. Earth itself has extremely coarse vibrations, and the sphere closest to the earth, let's call it the second, has "low" vibrations. The third has higher vibrations than the second, the fourth higher than the third, et cetera.

Many psychic investigators regard the lowest sphere in the afterlife as Hell, as it is very dark, hostile, unbelievably unpleasant. Individuals who function on a frequency of exceptionally low vibrations in terms of their level of spirituality, find themselves (when they die) in a sphere that functions on their level. Actually, spheres of a higher level will automatically reject entities—spirits—with lower vibrations.

But hell is NOT for eternity. Victor James Zammit, author of the book, *A Lawyer Presents The Case For The Afterlife: Irrefutable Objective Evidence,* explains that help is always available for any who ask for it and consistent with the Law of Progress, even the lowest spirit with the lowest vibrations (level of spirituality)—even if it takes eons of time—will one day progress to the higher spheres.

Here is how an eyewitness—the brilliant medium, Anthony Borgia, describes "Hell":

> Dimly, we could see through this miasma what might have been human beings, crawling like some foul beasts over the surface of the upper rocks. We could not think that they were human, but Edwin assured us that once they walked upon the earth place as men, that they had eaten and slept, and breathed the earthly air, had mixed with other men on earth. But they lived a life of spiritual foulness. In their death of the physical body they had gone to their true abode and their true estate in the spirit world.

(And describing the inhabitants in Hell):

> The hands were shaped like the talons of some bird of prey, with the finger nails so grown as to have become veritable claws. The face upon this monster was barely human, so

distorted was it, and malformed. The eyes were small and penetrating, but the mouth was huge and repulsive, with thick protruding lips set upon a prograthic jaw, and scarcely concealing the eeriest fangs of teeth...We gazed earnestly and long at this sorry wreck of what was once a human form and I wondered what earthly misdeeds had reduced it to this awful state of degeneration.

# NINE

## Soul Mates

How many times have we heard someone refer to his or her life partner as his or her "soul mate"? Since the effects of our past lives are mirrored in our present circumstances, our relationships are not as new as we would like to think. The memory of the soul and our past relationships shape our feelings toward them. As well, their memories of our actions during a past life influence how they react to us as well. Just as we see and understand life, so too does the soul; however, the soul sees with a memory that covers centuries of love and caring, hate and revenge, passion, et cetera. So whenever we feel an unfounded love or fondness for another, it is more than likely due to soul memories of the role that individual played in one of our past lives. As well, our unfounded dislike or revulsion toward another is based on their past actions against us or someone we loved. One must keep in mind that the influences of past-life actions are rarely clear-cut. Often, those individuals with whom we've had numerous good lives and relationships are the same people with whom we've had disagreements and arguments, in other words, a mix of good and bad. It is rare that a past life (much like the present) is without any disagreements whatsoever, but keep in mind that the more positive, well-developed areas from our past lives supply us with much pleasure and support in the present.

Conversely, those areas in which we did not have a proper focus do give us opportunities for pain and growth in our present relationships. It is simply impossible to avoid these influences as the Universal Law of Karma consistently brings before us the meeting of our past use of free will and consciousness. Thus, what we have done to other souls and they have done to us is reflected in the circumstances surrounding our present relationships and the basic, innate urges, attitudes and emotions we feel toward one another.

According to John Van Auken, Director of the Edgar Cayce Organization, A "soul mate" is merely a soul or souls with whom we have closely shared numerous lifetimes together, so many in fact, that we understand each other like no one else. This acquired understanding allows soul mates the ability to assist each other in ways that would be difficult (if not impossible) without the deep bonding that has occurred through the ages. Soul mates also have the distinct advantage of assisting each other to reach their highest potential as their deep inner knowing of each other allows them a distinct advantage. This doesn't necessarily mean they are duplicates that will agree on every issue, instead, they complement each other; each one bringing to the relationship what the other is missing, thereby forming a complete relationship and each one receiving more than they would alone.

Most people tend to think that the term "soul mates" automatically means lovers or marriage partners, but they can also be parents, children, siblings, friends, et cetera; although if they had been lovers in a former life there would be far too much magnetism for them to avoid a romantic encounter in their present life. On the other hand, if they had been family members or close friends in a former life, they would be more inclined toward a similar relationship in the present. A soul mate is definitely not always a sexual mate.

## TWIN SOULS

Since the soul possesses both male and female forces within itself prior to entering earth, it generally chooses one of its two sexual natures, projecting the unique characteristics of that sex while incarnate. Believe it or not, the sexual part of our soul that is unmanifested can actually incarnate the same time we do! In other words, our soul is capable of separating its dual sexual nature into two separate and distinct entities, one male, and the other female. Each of these two entities is able to incarnate into the earth at the same time in separate bodies that generally compliment the present sex. In other words, there is someone out there who is literally our other half—the other sexual aspect of our soul!

Edgar Cayce wrote that one of the more notable examples of this phenomenon was a group of four souls who, in their present incarnation, were husband, wife, eldest son and a female business associate who was also a very close friend of the family. The husband was told through the Casey readings that his present wife was his soul mate and his life would never have reached its fullest potential without her. As well, it went on to say that the female business associate and close family friend was his "twin soul"; in other words, she was the other sexual half of his complete soul. Even more amazing, his wife's twin soul was their eldest son! I can just picture the reader shaking his or her head in disbelief; however, the dynamics and dimensions of our lives are far greater than one could even hope to imagine.

Certainly not all cases are even close to this example from the Cayce readings as ordinarily the twin soul relationship is usually to be found amongst spouses, friends, parent and child and sometimes the twin soul isn't even incarnate at the same time. There is, however, a precedent that the majority of twin soul relationships follow. In their early incarnations together they tend to be lovers or mates. In later incarnations they tend to prefer a less sexually involved relationship, preferring a more work-related activity, particularly if the activity has a soul purpose. Whether this is due to the involution/evolution process where, in the earlier periods of descent into the world of the materialistic, they tend to continue their self-seeking, self-satisfying pursuits, but on the ascent toward a return to spirituality they steer more toward holistic relationships and purposes. This doesn't mean that every present sexual relationship is self-serving, however. From the Cayce material we find extremely healthy support for home and marriage plus all the natural sexual aspects that make up the union of two individuals in love and caring.

## PARENTS AND CHILDREN

As unbelievable as it seems, every soul actually chooses its parents. However, there is an exception. If a soul has abused, in any way, its gift of free will, then it comes under the powerful influence of the Universal Law and is carried along on the force of its past actions into present relationships that it must face up to. Keep in mind that no soul is given more than it can handle. This is not to say that it won't suffer; however, it won't be totally lost or destroyed by the burden of its karma.

Generally, however, a soul does choose its parents prior to entering the earth. There is no question that souls who have had familiarity together in past lives will be more attracted to each other than those who have had no past experience. This holds true even if they aren't particularly fond of each other. If the soul has a specific purpose for incarnating, and the majority of us do, then it will automatically be seeking those who are a part of fulfilling its purpose or those who can at least contribute to it. This in no way means that the childhood family life is all roses; in every relationship there are advantages and disadvantages, and one must accept the disadvantages in order to enjoy the advantages. As well, many times the disadvantages pave the road or create the opportunities for the advantages.

When a soul is deciding which channels (parents) would be most suitable for it to enter the world once again, it must accept the limitations of the family as well as the opportunities. There is no question that fate and destiny do exist, and the outcome of our past actions have an inertia that carries over into the present life and shapes it, thereby creating our destiny. However, absolutely nothing can surpass the power of the soul's free will. We are able to change directions at any time by using this free will. The incarnate parents also have a great influence as to which soul enters through them as their daily thoughts, actions, desires and purpose create a beacon of sorts for the souls that would respond to the same energies. This is particularly true of the mother as her daily activities and innermost thoughts during the gestation period create a magnetic field that attracts souls. Certainly more than one soul could wish to incarnate into the same family at the same time, however, the forces of cause and effect, will power and desire of the mother and the souls wishing to incarnate combine to make the final decision. Those souls who were not chosen for the present entry are likely to come in through another pregnancy if the opportunity is presented, thereby becoming the siblings of the souls who entered first; or they may incarnate into other families with whom blood relationships or friendships would naturally form and be maintained with the original channel family.

The soul generally enters the baby's body at or near the time of birth. In the Cayce readings there is an unusual case where the soul didn't enter until two days following the birth of the baby. When asked about the delay, Cayce responded that the soul was all too aware how very difficult life would be should it choose to enter and it wasn't too sure whether it wanted to go through with it! When Cayce was asked how the baby's body stayed alive for two days while the soul wrestled with its decision, he responded, "the spirit." According to Casey, the soul was the entity, with all its personal memories and aspirations and the spirit was the life force.

According to the metaphysical work of Rudolf Steiner, the soul actually incarnates in four stages. 1) A first level of consciousness enters at or near the time of birth; 2) A second and greater level of consciousness enters around the time the child cuts it first teeth; 3) A third level enters during puberty; and, 4) The final and complete entry of the soul occurs close to the age of twenty-one. Most sources agree that the first couple of years of life are primarily devoted to developing the physical body and that the years from two to seven shape much of the child's sense of self and its view of the world. In addition to the well-known physical and emotional changes that occur during the course of puberty, Cayce and other metaphysical sources add that this is the time when karmic influences begin to take hold, coinciding with the release of hormones.

This perspective sheds so much light on the otherwise baffling or incomprehensible changes in personality and behavior that sometimes accompany this stage of physical development. Around the age of twenty-one, the individual begins to assume its major course through life. Then, life progresses through a series of experiences and decision crossroads. These occur in natural and identifiable cycles, the most influential being the Seven Year Cycle: 1-7, 8-14, 15-21, 22-28, and so on. Notice how these cycles coincide with the general metaphysical cycles of: Birth; seven years of age; puberty (though puberty usually occurs before age fourteen, it is fulfilled at or near this age); and twenty-one years of age. Furthermore, each soul experiences life in two primary arenas: 1) The inner world of self, which includes one's mental and emotional being and physical body, and 2) The outer arena of life's unique circumstances, including the social, economic, racial, national and religious environment, all of which are generally set at birth and the outer world has pre-structured in specific ways.

In order for us to really understand how all of this occurs in life and relates to our own lives, let's look at some real-life examples.

Like most young girls, Linda Mills wanted to fall in love with a wonderful man, have a family and live a rich, full life. When she met her future husband, she was genuinely attracted to him, though she knew he wasn't everything she had dreamed about. She especially didn't like his tendency to make decisions for her. Nevertheless, their love for each other was strong and they felt a deep mutual attraction. An added joy was that they were quite comfortable with each other around their friends and family.

They married and had two daughters. For Linda, the first daughter was a joy. Throughout the pregnancy and after the birth, she and her new baby were very comfortable and happy with each other. They spent many wonderful hours together nursing and rocking while Linda softly hummed lullabies. But life with her second daughter was quite a different story. The pregnancy was uncomfortable, filled with sickness and stress, and after the birth she and the baby just never seemed to get into sync with each other. The baby didn't seem to enjoy being held or rocked like the first child and breastfeeding was a battle. In fact, the baby developed an allergy from the breast milk, and formula had to be substituted. Only the father's touch was comforting to this little one, and as she grew up her preference for him became even more evident. She was clearly "Daddy's little girl" while the first child was certainly Mommy's.

When this family received a past-life reading from Edgar Cayce, the cause of many of their present feelings and actions quickly surfaced. Apparently, Linda and her husband had been husband and wife before, but in the incarnation just prior to this one, they had been father and daughter, respectively. His tendency to make decisions for her and control her life was a carryover from being the father. In that past life Linda had been a rather wild and rebellious child. This was due in part to her resentment that the man who had been her equal in many lifetimes was now her father. It was a difficult life for him, too. Raising her was very hard, especially after the death of his wife in that lifetime. Naturally, all of these feelings carried over into their present life and marriage.

As for the children, the first daughter had been Linda's close friend through many lifetimes, bringing this love and friendship into the present life. In their most recent past life, the first daughter had helped Linda deal with the problems Linda had had with her father (Linda's present husband), and now as their daughter, she would do so again. Now, the second daughter had been the father's lover in many past lives; so you can just imagine the mutual enmity this created between the mother and daughter in the present. Linda's milk wasn't all the baby was allergic to! Neither did she want Linda's love and comfort as much as she did her father's. The father and his second daughter would have to learn to love each other in a much different way or break one of the strictest taboos, incest. All of these feelings were occurring subconsciously, of course, subtly affecting the conscious life.

As we can see, the deep currents of past experiences were playing a significant role in their present relationships. According to the Cayce readings, their goal now, from their souls' point of view, was to live together again and make an effort to accentuate the love and virtues, and minimize the resentments and bad habits they carried with them as a result of their past.

In another case, despite all his efforts to ignore or resist it, Michael Parks was afraid of the dark. His fear of the dark was not like most children's; he was deathly afraid, to the point of suffocating if left in the dark too long. As far as he and his parents could recall, his childhood was rather normal and nothing had occurred that might have caused this fear. Yet, during all of his childhood life in his parent's home, anyone in charge of him had to be aware of his fear and take precautions to insure that he was never inadvertently left alone in a dark room or house. His parents were very tolerant of his fear, caring for him in every way and were unusually understanding and sympathetic. And later, when he married and started a home and family of his own, his wife assumed the burden of his fear. She too proved to be very patient with him. Together they worked out an elaborate scheme whereby he could go to bed with the lights on and she would come to bed after he had fallen asleep. Only then would she turn the lights off so she could fall asleep. Even so, if he awoke during the night, he would become extremely anxious and uncomfortable. He would have to fight to keep himself from panicking before turning on his bedside light. But once the light was on, the only way he could get back to sleep was to go into the living room, turn on all the lights and sleep on the couch, knowing the lights would be on while he slept.

One night Michael awoke from a terrifying dream, a dream that was to be the beginning of his conquering the fear. He dreamt he was in a dark dungeon surrounded by wet, stone walls that went up so high he couldn't see where they ended. There was absolutely no way out and no one was coming to help him. As he stood there he began to cry. He cried so long and hard that the cell began to fill with his tears. When he noticed the tear-water was up to his chest, he tried to stop crying but couldn't get hold of himself—it all seemed too horribly fixed, so unchangeable that he felt completely trapped without hope of ever seeing light or life again.

Eventually, the pool of tears reached his nose and he had to stand on his tiptoes to breathe, yet he continued to cry. Slowly, he allowed himself to ease under the water, drifting into a sorrowful, lonely dream of letting go, surrendering his will to the reality of his predicament. At this point he awoke from the dream. The sheets were soaked and his body was covered with chilly sweat. When he told his wife and parents the dream they cried and were very upset by it. However, underneath, Michael was beginning to feel pretty good. In fact, he noticed his fear of the dark had actually diminished since the dream. It was as though something in that dream had healed and changed him. About a year later, Michael happened to take part in a series of exercises for recalling past-life experiences. From the information he received during these exercises and several more dreams over the next two years, he began to understand why he was afraid of the dark.

In a previous incarnation he had been a renegade from the courts and causes of Louis XIV. So violent and disruptive were his counterattacks against the king that he became one of the most wanted men in France. His raids destroyed many of the king's storehouses, and his ability to elude capture created a great deal of hatred among the king's soldiers charged with capturing him. One day they did capture him, and in retaliation for his actions and also as a result of their frustration with trying to stop him, they threw him into the bottom of a well-like dungeon, covered it and left him there to die a slow death. In this terrible place of complete darkness he managed to survive for several days. In the beginning he was sure his friends and his wife would come to his rescue. But as time went by, he realized that no one was coming and he lost hope and died. In the latter days of his ordeal he lost all sense of time and his mind began to fall apart. He could no longer be sure of what was real and what was illusion. But the worst part was the unrelenting darkness and confinement. This was what his soul remembered and most feared.

Just as we might expect, his current parents and wife, who helped him deal with his fear in the present life, had been the very people he had counted on to rescue him from the dungeon. His father and his wife had been his close friends and colleagues-in-arms, while his present mother had been his wife in the French incarnation. They didn't go to his rescue because he had become so notorious that it would have been too risky to attempt to save him without being captured and thrown into the dungeon with him. To a great degree, his own actions had brought him to this end; yet his parents and wife regretted that they had not at least tried to rescue him. His present-life dream was too much for his parents and wife to hear without deeply reacting to his ordeal. However, Michael's reliving the experience in his dream somehow released him from his life-long fear of the dark.

In yet another less dramatic case, a man who had fallen in love with a divorcée found himself struggling with his feelings. He eventually married her and tried to be the best stepfather to her child he possibly could; but when he discovered that he could not father children himself, he felt cheated and fought feelings of resentment toward the special relationship between his wife and her child. When he received a past-life reading from Edgar Cayce, he was told that in a previous incarnation in ancient Greece he had been married to the same woman. In that life, she was the one unable to conceive a child. Though aware of her sadness and heightened sensitivity because of the added implications of being barren in those days, he chose a second wife to bear him a child. He further shamed and humiliated her by bringing the second wife and child to live in the same house, forcing her to witness the open joy and affection expressed in the little family.

In his present-life circumstances, according to Cayce, he was merely meeting himself: though he deeply desired his own offspring, he was impotent; and though living in his own home, he felt like an outsider to the love shared within it. Taking advantage of the present situation and making life as miserable as possible for her husband would simply be setting herself up for a future destiny of sadness. The law of karma is very impersonal: what one does, one experiences, without exception. If this woman now chose to help her husband meet his fate as best she could, she would heal many wounds and free herself at the same time.

In still another case, a beautiful woman from the modern cosmopolitan life of a big city came to Cayce and described her tragic predicament, asking for a remedy. Her present husband was impotent and she was a beautiful woman in the prime of her life. Why? Why was she in such a tragic situation? She lamented. She went on to say that there was another man she knew at work, and she wondered if she could have an affair with him yet remain with her husband...because she did love her husband; she simply wanted to fulfill all of her womanhood.

Cayce responded by showing her why she was faced with such a dilemma. In a past incarnation during the Crusades, she and her present husband were also married to each other. He was then one of the greatest of the Crusaders, often going off to war. However, every time he left, he saw to it that she wore a chastity belt, literally putting her under lock and key! Then and there she swore deep in her heart she would get even with him, and now, Cayce said, she had him right where she'd always wanted him—in a position where she could make him pay dearly. What a triangle! I wouldn't be surprised if the other man had also been hanging around the castle while the rest of the men were off to war. At any rate, here they were again, set up perfectly to play out resolution or revenge for past actions with each other. The husband had used his free will to squash his wife's, forcing her to submit to his sexual restraints without any choice on her part. Now he found himself sexually restricted and frustrated, and completely subject to her will and her choices. She now had the power to make him pay. Paradoxically, she also found herself wanting to make a success of her marriage and her home, and despite his past wrong, she loved her husband, and he returned that love in so many ways. If only he were able to sexually fulfill her! What a tangled web. The choice was completely hers; nothing was standing in her way.

Cayce advised her to do whatever she would want done to her if she were in her husband's shoes, and she did. She withdrew from the other man's affections and built a loving home with her husband. We might well feel that she suffered twice in the relationship, but if she had only not wanted revenge on him, she wouldn't have had to be with him again. The true karma was within him. She got involved again by her desire to get even with him. No doubt she will eventually incarnate into a life filled with physical, mental, emotional and spiritual happiness and the rest of the world will probably look at her and think she is lucky rather than deserving.

One example of how past lives can affect non-family relationships is that of a businessman who happened to receive many readings from Edgar Cayce. In fact, these readings are just phenomenal in what they reveal "behind the scenes," so to speak, in illustrating what profound effects past-life experiences and emotions have on present relationships, and in this case, on a "typical" business meeting:

When Walter Morrison walked into a board meeting, he was walking into a history that reached far beyond his present life. Amid the members of this board were souls who had been his conquerors, his servants, his concubines, his cohorts and his bitter enemies! Imagine what the underlying motivations were when Walter made a proposal which the group had to vote on, or when Walter had to cast his vote concerning a proposal by one of the other members of this band of souls. Who among the group would tend to support him? Who would tend to thwart his efforts and ideas? And whom would he tend to support and resist? Many of these answers are predictable based on their past-life experiences with each other; experiences that they would innately respond to on a soul level because of their past affinities and antipathies for one another.

Walter himself was curiously amazed at how well the past-life readings predicted his present feelings for various members of the board. Only in a few cases did he find he really didn't have any particular innate reaction to a member. And in most cases, the members that consistently rubbed him the wrong way were those who had been on his bad side in past lives, and those that seemed to agree and support him consistently were those who had done so in the past.

When relationships are viewed with a past-life perspective, the dynamics of the behavior, including the attitudes and emotions in a relationship, become more than just current moodiness or general personality traits. There are undercurrents of memory that simply cannot easily be ignored.

## GROUP RELATIONSHIPS

The same principals just discussed apply to group relationships as well. From Day One, all our souls have traveled together creating forces of magnetism that assist to maintain and build on these group relationships. The majority of souls on earth have been together in past ages of human history. In other words, the type of relationships among the world's population today is a direct result of their past lives with each other. The souls who entered this planetary system, entering the realms of consciousness in this region of the cosmos consist of our largest soul group. This group can then be separated into subgroups called "the generations," containing souls who travel through the natural cycles of their lives on earth together, which can be divided further into the numerous nations, races, cultures, religions, et cetera, that have formed during eons of interaction together.

Within these groups are the subgroups of souls who share similar purposes, ideas, philosophies, attitudes and aspirations. From here, the soul groups further divide into numerous smaller groups of personal relationships communities, families, businesses, teams schools and so on. Soul groups create an affinity among their members by not only the cumulative experiences they share, but also through their collective memory of how life has been for them and what they have come to mutually desire out of it. In a manner of speaking, such groups form a distinct collective consciousness and spirit, much like the souls who gave us "the spirit of '76," reflecting that soul group's mutual hopes, attitudes, purposes and memories.

Soul groups are neither rigid nor static. Any individual soul can use its free will to seek an experience in another group. There are many cases of souls changing political allegiance, race, or religion from one lifetime to another. Neither do the generations incarnate in strict, rigid patterns. A member of one generation may enter again with another generation. For example, two members of a family group who were father and son in one life may change positions and become son and father in another, or grandfather and grandson. They may even choose to be in the same generation in an incarnation as brothers, for example. However, they may choose not to be in the same family again.

Although soul groups are fairly well established and have significant pull on the individuals within them, they do not have greater influence than an individual soul's will to change. Generally, however, soul groups cycle in and out of the Earth together and, therefore, at approximately the same time. (I am speaking in eras and ages, not days or years.) This is particularly evident in the past-life readings of Edgar Cayce. Many of them were for souls who fell into one of the two major soul groups and naturally followed their cycles of incarnation.

# TEN

## Beginnings of Parapsychology

Throughout history there have been persistent tales of those who possessed the ability to read the minds of others as well as foretell the future and observe spirits and ghosts. The bible is filled with accounts of those whose dreams told of future events as well. The ancient Romans and Greeks consulted their official oracles and refused to pursue any important undertaking without first consulting the pythoness at Delphi or the Sybilline prophecies. Ancient Greeks and Romans employed official oracles and no important undertaking would be pursued without consulting the pythoness at Delphi or the Sybilline prophecies. During the Middle Ages there were numerous stories of saints and prophets who had visions and mystical experiences. During the nineteenth century, the belief in the paranormal retained its popularity, and by the early twentieth century, at a time when the majority of people began to think of psychic experiences as sheer nonsense, a modern type of scientific study began its research into the validity of psychic phenomenon. It was termed "Parapsychology."

Henry Sidgwick, a professor of philosophy at Cambridge University, was the first to undertake serious enquiries into spiritualism. As well as exposing a number of fraudulent mediums, he founded the Society for Psychical Research (SPR) in 1882, becoming its first president. Other early members were, William Barrett, Professor of physics at Dublin University; Sir Oliver Lodge, professor of physics at Liverpool University; the classic scholar Walter Leaf; and a man with clairvoyant abilities called Alfred Balfour, who would later become the Prime Minister of Britain.

The society's goal was to investigate psychic phenomena objectively and scientifically: "to examine without prejudice or prepossession and in a scientific spirit those faculties of man, real or supposed, which appear to be inexplicable on any generally recognized hypothesis." The phenomena to be investigated included the influence of one mind over another such as, hypnotism, clairvoyance, spiritualism and ghosts. The Society has since investigated literally thousands of cases, and an American branch was started following Sir William Barrett's tour of the United States in 1885.

The validity of psychic research as a science continued to flourish when, in 1920, William McDougall, president of the British Society for Psychical Research, was appointed head of the psychology department at Harvard University in the United States, and as a result gained funding in order to carry on his psychical researches. In 1927, McDougall was transferred to Duke University where Joseph Rhine, a botanist and research assistant, joined him. Rhine had developed an avid interest in psychic research following a lecture he attended by Sir Arthur Conan Doyle, author of the Sherlock Holmes stories and an avid and committed spiritualist as well.

Pioneers in the field of psychic research, Dr. Rhine (along with his wife, Louisa) delved into their research with rigorous scientific methodology. It was they who introduced the term ESP (extrasensory perception) to describe the ability possessed by those who are able to acquire information otherwise unavailable to the known five senses, describing this ability as "a two-way exchange with the environment that is not mediated by the senses and muscles." Professor Rhine was the originator of the term "Parapsychology" (literally, *beyond psychology*) in an attempt to establish the fact that his discipline was scientific, but which he defined as "the study and investigation of phenomena that are not explainable by known natural laws."

There was certainly no lack of incoming reports of psychic phenomena; however, the researchers dilemma was the ability to gain proof by way of repeatable experiments. For example: How does one encourage a ghost to show up at the laboratory for testing? And though someone has the ability to predict the future, would the testing under strict laboratory conditions stifle that gift? Rhine and his team developed various methods of testing psychokinesis (PK) and ESP by employing statistical analysis. For example, the overall number of guesses of hits exceeded the chance rate of scoring by a significantly large margin.

Another experiment they employed in order to test psychokinesis (or moving objects with the mind), was measuring the success of subjects in their attempts to influence the fall of dice by calling out the face required before the dice was thrown. Not surprisingly, some of the scores rated far above the statistical average.

Since psychic phenomena have remained inexplicable in terms of physics and biology, Rhine was subjected to a great deal of criticism from his fellow scientists and other psychologists following the release of his book, *Extra Sensory Perception,* in 1934. Rhine refined his techniques and published *New Frontier of the Mind* in 1937 and *The Reach of the Mind* in 1947, thereby confirming his belief of ESP.

The criticism continued, however, even to the point where he was falsely accused of conspiring with his subjects to fake results. Rhine maintained that simply because the demonstrable existence of psi abilities could not be proven perhaps a re-thinking of science was in order. He argued that there must be a "non-physical determinant in the mental life of man," and that the human organism operated far above the mere mechanical model presumed by biologists. He was also of the belief that the phenomenon of psi ability is within everyone as opposed to the belief that it is ingrained in just a few select individuals. He further maintained his original interest in the survival of consciousness following death in that it existed as an "extra-biological" dimension.

## TERMS DEFINED

Parapsychologists coined new terms to categorize the phenomena they investigated, and these rapidly gained currency amongst both psychics and the general public. Below are some of the most commonly used terms:

**Clairaudience:** "Clear Hearing." In this instance, the psychic "hears" extrasensory information about objects and events.

**Clairsentience:** "Clear Knowing" or "Clear Awareness." This general term covers clairaudience, clairvoyance and other such extrasensory methods of gaining information.

**Clairvoyance:** "Clear Seeing." The extrasensory perception of objects and events whereby the clairvoyant "sees" information in a visual form. Clairvoyance is distinct from telepathy, when information is plucked from the mind of the sitter, and from mediumship where the spirits of the dead gives information.

**ESP:** "Extrasensory Perception." The acquiring information without the use of the accepted five senses. The term is often used to cover the whole gamut of psi abilities and phenomena.

**Ganzfeld:** "Whole Field." This technique is used to deprive the subject of sensory stimulation by covering the eyes, using white noise, etc. This has been found to increase psi and metal imagery, perhaps because the mind is forced to look inwards for stimulation. The technique was first used (independently) by researchers William Braud, Chuck Horton and Adrian Parker.

**Mediums/mediumship:** Mediums claim to communicate with the spirits of the dead, often while in a trance-like state, and pass on messages from them. This should not be confused with clairvoyance or telepathy. The Rhines investigated a medium at Duke University in a double blind test. The medium successfully obtained information about a sitter in an adjoining room, but the problem for the Rhines was how to determine and prove whether the information was passed on by a discarnate spirit, or simply via telepathy or clairvoyance.

**Paranormal:** "Beyond Normal" or phenomena not explainable by known natural laws.

**Parapsychology:** "Beyond Psychology." A scientific discipline that examines those experiences and phenomena that are unexplainable in terms of accepted science, but which uses accepted scientific methodology to examine them. The study deals with mental phenomena, but excludes fortune telling, magic, astrology, palmistry, etc.

**Precognition:** "Knowing Before" or the extrasensory perception of future events, i.e. knowing something before it happens. Such information is often gained by the subject in a dream, while daydreaming or in a trance-like state. Abraham Lincoln is said to have dreamt of himself in his coffin a few days before he was assassinated. There are many stories of people not boarding planes because they dreamt of a crash, or of people who foresaw the death of relatives. These instances of precognition concerning very specific and definite events are distinct from the general and vague trend predictions of of most astrologers and tarot readers.

**Psi:** After initial efforts to isolate the various types of parapsychical abilities such as PK clairvoyance, precognition and telepathy, many researchers concluded they were as the effects of a single ability they called psi, after the Greek letter. The term was introduced by Thouless and Wiesner in 1948 and was at first divided into two categories called "psi-kappa" for active psi such as PK and "psi-gamma" for passive psi, such as telepathy. Psi is sometimes used interchangeably with the term ESP or psychic, though parapsychologists prefer the term psi to psychic.

**Psychic:** Someone who regularly uses or who has psi abilities.

**Psychokinesis or PK:** "Movement by Mind" or the ability to influence the environment with thought alone. Gamblers have often believed that when they were in a lucky state of mind they could influence the roll of dice or spin of a roulette wheel. Rhine was interested in the incidents of apparent hauntings by poltergeists and suggested that these may have resulted from unconscious PK activity from disturbed individuals. Rhine thought that while ESP was analogous to paranormal sensory functioning, PK was analogous to paranormal motor functioning. The term psychokinesis was introduced by Rhine, and later divided by researchers into macro-PK where the results are readily witnessed, such as in the fall of a dice or the movement of a pendulum, etc. and micro-PK where the results are only detectable by statistical analysis. The latter might include influencing microphysical targets, perhaps electrical or atomic processes such as the emanation of electrons from radioactive substances.

The influencing of moving targets such as the dice is called PK-MT; static targets, PK-ST; and living targets, PK-LT or bio-PK. The latter might include affecting the growth of vegetation and may account for the uncanny ability of some people to produce lush plant—the so-called green fingered folks—while others produce mediocre specimens. Bio-

PK might also conceivably have effects on animal tissue and play a part healing abilities.

**Sensitives:** A general term for clairvoyants and mediums, those with more developed psi abilities.

**Spiritualism:** A religious movement based on communication with spirits of the dead through sensitives called mediums. It began in 1848 when two New York girls called Margaret and Kate Fox enthralled the nation with accounts of "spirit rappings," which they claimed were messages from the dead. Interest in spiritualism steadily grew and reached a peak during the First World War.

**Telekinesis:** "Remote movement" is an alternative term for psychokinesis.

**Telepathy:** "Remote speaking" or "feeling/perception at a distance" is the ability to transmit or receive information from one mind to another, which might be defined as mind-to-mind speaking. Many people experience the feeling of knowing who is on the other end of a ringing telephone, while mothers can often sense when their distant children are in danger or distress. Testing and proving telepathy, as distinct from other psi abilities, has proved difficult, since in all cases the subject might have obtained information clairvoyantly as well as telepathically.

**Thoughtography:** The causing of an image, by projection of thought, onto an unexposed photographic plate. Some famous experiments were conducted with psychic Ted Serios who seemed to be able to "project" an image onto unexposed film, which would appear once it was developed.

## STATES OF CONSCIOUSNESS

The state of a subject's mind at the time of testing seems to influence the outcome of the experiment. ESP experiences rarely occur in a normal, waking state of mind. Experimenters found that better results were obtained from those in what might be called an altered state of consciousness (ASC)—a very relaxed state, in a mild trance, daydreaming, or just feeling detached or abstracted. Consciously trying too hard proved counter-productive.

# Glossary

## Terms and Explanations

**Absent Healing:**      Healing that takes place when the healer is not in direct contact with the individual to be healed.

**Absent Healer:**      A person, not present during a session, on whose behalf readings are given.

**Acupuncture:**      Traditional Chinese medical practice that involves sticking needles into specific locations on the body. See also **Healing**.

**Agent:**      a) A person who attempts to communicate information to another in an ESP experiment; b) The subject in a psychokinesis experiment; c) An individual who is the focus of poltergeist activity.

**Akashic Records:**      "Memories" of all experiences since the beginning of time, believed by some mystical doctrines to be stored permanently in a spiritual substance.

**Alien Abduction Experience:**      Reported experiences of being abducted by alien creatures, often into spacecraft. Abductees often experience lost time and suffer loss of memory. When memories are recovered, often using hypnotic regression, abductees may report that surgical operations were performed on them.

**Alpha Rhythm:**      Electrical activity in the brain (about 10 cycles per second) associated with a state of mental relaxation.

| | |
|---|---|
| **Altered State of Consciousness:** | A term used to refer to any state of consciousness that is different from "normal" states of waking of sleeping. ASC's include hypnosis, trance, ecstasy, psychedelic and meditative experience. ASC's do not necessarily have paranormal features. |
| **Ancestor Worship:** | Religious practices involving veneration of dead ancestors. |
| **Angels:** | Benevolent spiritual beings who help people in need. |
| **Animal Magnetism:** | A term coined by F.A. Mesmer to refer to a putative force or fluid capable of being transmitted from one person to another, producing healing effects. |
| **Animal Mutilation:** | Refers to cases in which animal corpses (often cattle) have been found with bizarre injuries that do not seem to have a normal explanation in terms of illness, accident or action of predators. Cuts and injuries often appear to have been carried out with surgical precision. Typically, the corpse is drained of blood. Certain body parts may be absent (e.g., genitals). |
| **Animal psi:** | Paranormal abilities exhibited by animals. Also known as "Anpsi." |
| **Animism:** | Religious practices based on the belief that all living things and natural objects have their individual spiritual essence or soul. |
| **Announcing Dream:** | A dream believed to announce an individual's rebirth. |

| | |
|---|---|
| **Anomalous Experience:** | A general term referring to unusual experiences that can't be explained in terms of current scientific knowledge. |
| **Anomalous Phenomena:** | Natural phenomena that cannot be explained in terms of current scientific knowledge. |
| **Apparition:** | A visual appearance (hallucination) often of a person or scene, generally experienced in a waking or hypnagogic or hynopompic state. |
| **Apport:** | A physical object which appears in a way that cannot be explained (seeming to come from nowhere). Apports are often associated with the séance room and physical mediumship. |
| **Artefact:** | In parapsychology, false evidence of paranormal phenomena, due to some extraneous normal influence. |
| **Astral Body:** | A term used by occultists to refer to a "double" of a person's physical body and is believed to be separable from the physical body during "astral projection" and/or at death. |
| **Astral Projection:** | A term used by parapsychologists and theosophists for "Out-of-Body Experiences." |
| **Atavism:** | Re-emergence of ancestral characteristics; a genetic throwback. |
| **Automatic Writing:** | The ability to write intelligible messages without conscious control or knowledge of what is being written. |

| | |
|---|---|
| **Automatism:** | Physical activities such as arm movements, writing, drawing, musical performance that occur without the automatist's conscious control or knowledge. Also known as "motor automatism." |
| **Autoscopy:** | Seeing one's double or looking back at one's own body from a position outside of the body. |
| **Ba:** | Ancient Egyptian concept of a person's essence, believed to be immortal. |
| **Banchee:** | In Gaelic belief, a female entity who heralds a death by groaning and screaming. |
| **Bardo:** | In Tibetan Buddhism, an intermediate state of existence, usually referring to the state between life and rebirth. |
| **Bilocation:** | Being, or appearing to be, in two places at the same time. |
| **Cerebral Anoxia:** | Lack of oxygen to the brain, often causing sensory distortions and hallucinations. |
| **Channeling:** | Receiving messages and inspiration from discarnate entities. |
| **Clairaudience:** | The paranormal obtaining of information by hearing sounds or voices. |
| **Clairvoyance:** | A general term that refers to the paranormal obtaining of information about an object or event. (In modern usage.) |
| **Coincidence:** | The occurrence, within a short space of time, of two or more meaningfully related events and without any apparent casual connection between them. Coincidences are sometimes bizarre and extraordinarily improbable. |

| | |
|---|---|
| **Collective Apparition:** | Concept put forward by Carl Jung to refer to a level of unconscious thought and experience shared collectively by humans. |
| **Contact Mind Reading:** | In which the "mind reader" (who generally holds a hand or arm) responds to slight muscle movements produced unconsciously by the person whose mind is being read. |
| **Corn Circle:** | Elaborate formations found in growing crops, most commonly in Southern Britain. Many of these formations appear to have been intelligently created and to have some symbolic meaning. |
| **Cosmic Consciousness:** | A blissful experience in which the person becomes aware of the whole universe as a living being. |
| **Crisis Apparition:** | In which an individual is seen within a few hours of an important crisis such as death, an accident or a sudden illness. |
| **Cross-Correspondence:** | Items of information, received independently by two or more mediums, which make sense when pieced together. |
| **Crystal Gazing:** | Staring into a reflecting surface such as a mirror, glass, crystal or liquid in order to obtain paranormal information, also known as "scrying." |
| **Daemon:** | A guardian spirit who communicates inspiration and advice. |
| **Deathbed Experience:** | A dying person's awareness of deceased friends and relatives. |
| **Déjà vu:** | An individual's awareness that current events have been experienced before. |

| | |
|---|---|
| **Dematerialization:** | The paranormal fading or disappearance of a physical object. |
| **Demonic Possession:** | Possession by evil spirits. |
| Depot: | The paranormal movements of objects out of a secure, enclosed space. |
| **Direct Voice:** | A voice heard in a séance, which does not seem to emanate from any person. The voice may seem to come out of thin air, or from a trumpet. |
| **Discarnate Entity:** | Often referred to as the spirit or personality of a deceased individual. |
| **Disassociation:** | Activity performed outside of normal conscious awareness or mental processes that suggest the existence of separate centers of consciousness. |
| **Divining Rod:** | A forked rod (or sometimes a pair of Y-shaped rods) used in dowsing. |
| **Doppleganger:** | A mirror image or "double" of an individual. |
| **Dowsing:** | The paranormal detection of underground water, mineral deposit, lost objects or individuals using a divining rod. |
| **Earthquake Effect:** | A phenomenon produced by a physical medium involving a room shaking as if there was an earthquake. |
| **Ectoplasm:** | A semi-fluid substance exuded by some physical mediums often materializing into familiar faces or objects. |
| **Elongation:** | Paranormal extension of the physical body, reported by some mystics. |
| **Evil Eye:** | Alleged ability of some individuals to harm others by merely looking at them. |

| | |
|---|---|
| **Exorcism:** | A religious or quasi-religious rite to drive out evil spirits. |
| **Extrasensory Perception:** | Paranormal acquisition of information that includes clairvoyance, telepathy and precognition. |
| **False Awakening:** | An experience in which an individual believes he or she has woken up, but actually is still dreaming. |
| **Fire Walking:** | Walking on red-hot coals without pain or damage to feet. |
| **Focal Person:** | An individual who is the focus or at the center of poltergeist activity. |
| **Glossolalia:** | Unintelligible speech generally uttered in a trance. Also known as "speaking in tongues." |
| **Guardian Angel:** | A spirit believed to protect an individual. |
| **Haunting:** | Paranormal phenomena such as apparitions, unexplained sights sounds, smells or other sensations that are associated over a lengthy period of time with a specific location. |
| **Healing:** | Generally indicates cures that cannot be explained in terms of accepted medical practices and principles. |
| **Hyperaesthesia:** | An exceptionally acute sensory awareness. |
| **Hypnogogic Imagery:** | Occurring in the hypnogogic state. (Occurs while waking up.) |
| **Incorruptibility:** | An inexplicable lack of decay in a corpse. |
| **Indirect Voice:** | Phenomenon in which the discarnate entity appears to speak using the vocal apparatus of the medium. Often the voice will sound entirely different from the medium's natural voice. |

| | |
|---|---|
| **Intuition:** | The paranormal ability to grasp the elements of a situation or to draw conclusions about complex events in ways that go beyond a purely rational or intellectual analysis. |
| **Ka:** | Ancient Egyptian term for the double. |
| **Karma:** | Hindu and Buddhist ethical doctrine of "as one sows, so shall one reap." |
| **Kirlian Photography:** | A photographic method involving high frequency electric current, discovered by SD & V Kirlian in the Soviet Union Kirlian photography often show coloured halos or "auras" surrounding subjects or objects. |
| **Laying on of Hands:** | A healing practice in which the healer's hands are placed near the body of the sick person. |
| **Levitation:** | The paranormal raising or suspension of an object or individual. |
| **Life Review:** | Flashback memories of the whole of a person's life, often associated with the "Near-Death Experience." |
| **Lucid Dreaming:** | Dreaming in which the individual is aware that the experience is a dream often associated with feelings of aliveness and freedom and the ability to control the dream events. |
| **Lycanthropy:** | The transformation of a person into the form of a wolf, also known as "shape-shifting." |
| **Mantra:** | A sacred sound or sacred syllables used in meditation. |
| **Materialization:** | The formation of a visible and tangible object or human shape during a séance. |

| | |
|---|---|
| **Meditation:** | Mental or physical-mental techniques that aim to produce spiritually desirable states of consciousness. |
| **Medium:** | An individual who acts as an intermediary between discarnate entities. |
| **Mesmerism:** | A system of healing developed by FA Mesmer, involving the induction of trance states and the transfer of animal magnetism. Individuals in a Mesmeric trance often show paranormal abilities such as clairvoyance. |
| **Metal Bending:** | The ability to bend metal objects A phenomenon made popular by Uri Geller. |
| **Multiple Personality:** | A psychiatric condition in which an individual manifests two or more distinct and separate personalities at different times. |
| **Mystic:** | An individual who has mystical experiences. |
| **Near-Death Experience:** | Experiences of individuals after they have been pronounced dead, or have been very close to death Typical features of the NDE arc a tunnel experience, light, seeing dead friends and relatives, experiencing a divine and loving presence, and making a choice (or being told) to return. NDE's can be frightening and depressing but often have a profound effects on the individual's life. |
| **Numerology:** | A system of divination involving the interpretation of numbers. |
| **Occultism:** | Esoteric systems of belief and practice that assume the existence of mysterious forces and entities. |
| **Omen:** | A sign that foretells events. |

| | |
|---|---|
| **Ouija Board:** | A board with letters and numbers on which messages are spelled out by unconsciously moving with fingers, a glass or planchette. (Read more about ouija boards and the danger they present at the end of this Glossary.) |
| **Out-of-Body Experience:** | A fully conscious experience in which the individual's center of awareness appears to be outside of the physical body. |
| **Palmistry:** | The art of assessing an individual's character and forecasting life events by examining features of the hand. |
| **Paranormal:** | Beside or beyond the normal, inexplicable in terms of our ordinary understanding or current scientific knowledge. |
| **Paranormal Dreams:** | Dreams in which the dream imagery produces paranormal knowledge. |
| **Parapsychology:** | Term coined by J.B. Rhine to refer to the experimental and quantitive study of paranormal phenomena, now generally used instead of "psychical research" to refer to all scientific investigation of the paranormal. |
| **Past Life Memories:** | Mental images that are believed to be memories of previous lives. |
| **Phrenology:** | The reading of character and mental ability from the shape of an individual's skull. |

| | |
|---|---|
| **Poltergeist:** | A German word meaning "noisy" or "trouble-some" spirit. Poltergeist activity may include unexplained noises, movements of objects, outbreaks of fire, floods, pricks or scratches to a person's body. Unlike hauntings, which are associated with specific locations, pol-tergeists typically, though not always, focus on a person who is often a young child or an adolescent. |
| **Possession:** | Refers to cases in which an individual's body is apparently taken over by another personal-ity or entity. |
| **Precognition:** | The paranormal awareness of future events. |
| **Pre-Existence:** | Belief that the personality or soul exists prior to birth. |
| **Premonition:** | An experience that foretells future events. |
| **Presence:** | A subjective feeling that a person, animal or discarnate entity is present. |
| **Prophecy:** | Prediction, usually resulting from a sense of spiritual revelation. |
| **Psi (psi):** | A term used to encompass all paranormal activities. |
| **Psyche:** | Generally refers to the mind. |
| **Psychical Research:** | A term coined in the late 19th century to refer to the scientific study of the paranormal, now largely superceded by "parapsychology." |
| **Psychokinesis:** | The paranormal influence of the mind on physical events and processes. |
| **Psychometry:** | Obtaining paranormal knowledge using a physical object as a focus. Also known as "Object Reading." |

| | |
|---|---|
| **Raps:** | The name given to unexplained knocking sounds associated with physical mediumship. |
| **Rebirth:** | In Buddhism, the belief that there is some continuity of mind from one lifetime to the next. |
| **Regression:** | A technique used in hypnosis involving past lives. |
| **Reincarnation:** | The belief that some aspect of a person's being, be it consciousness, personality, or soul, survives death. |
| **Retrocognition:** | Paranormal knowledge of past events. |
| **Shaman:** | A medicine man or woman who communicates with spirits while in a trance. May also show other paranormal abilities. |
| **Shape-Shifting:** | Paranormal ability to assume the form of another individual, animal or entity. |
| **Simultaneous Dreams:** | A dream containing elements that correspond closely with those of another individual. |
| **Sleep Paralysis:** | An often-frightening state of seeming to be awake, but unable to move. |
| **Spectre:** | A ghost. |
| **Spirit Cure:** | Healing that is believed to result from the intervention of spirits. |
| **Spontaneous Human Combustion:** | Refers to cases in which a badly burned human body has been discovered in circumstances suggesting that the fire originated spontaneously in or on the body of the victim. |
| **Stigmata**: | Unexplained markings on an individual's body that correspond to the wounds of Christ. |

| | |
|---|---|
| **Table Tilting:** | Mysterious movements of a table, usually occurring during a séance. Often the movements are interpreted as spirit communications. |
| **Telekinesis:** | Paranormal movement of objects. |
| **Telepathy:** | Paranormal awareness of another's experience, thoughts and feelings. In practice it is difficult to distinguish between telepathy and clairvoyance. |
| **Teleportation:** | Paranormal transportation of objects to a distant place. |
| **Thoughtography:** | Paranormal ability to produce images on photographic film by concentrating on a mental image. Most famously demonstrated by Ted Serios. |
| **Transpersonal Psychology:** | The study of experiences, beliefs and practices that suggest that the sense of self can extend beyond our personal or individual reality. The subject matter of transpersonal psychology overlaps to some extent with "Parapsychology," but the two disciplines tend to have different approaches and emphasis:<br><br>Parapsychology is primarily concerned with the investigation of evidence for and against the reality of paranormal phenomena.<br><br>Transpersonal Psychology, on the other hand, is more interested in investigating the significance of such phenomena. (For example: the ways in which they may give individuals a sense of connectedness with a larger, more universal or spiritual reality.) |

| | |
|---|---|
| **Verdical Dream:** | A dream that corresponds to real events (past, present or future) that are unknown to the dreamer. |
| **Xenoglossy:** | The ability to speak or write in a language that has never been learned. |
| **Yoga:** | Religious philosophy originating in India advocating the use of physical and psycho-spiritual techniques to lead an individual to higher consciousness. |

# On a Final Note

## The Dangers of the Ouija Board

Ouija boards have been around as long as I can remember, and though the board itself is not dangerous, the form of communication required can very well be! Why? Simply put, the majority of spirits contacted through the Ouija are from the "lower astral plane." As a rule, these spirits have died a sudden or violent death, either by their own hand (suicide) or due to murder, and they are often confused. Therefore, many violent, negative and potentially dangerous conditions are present to those using the board. Sometimes more than one spirit will attempt to come through at the same time, but the real danger lies when you ask for physical proof of their existence! You might say, "Well, if you're really a spirit, then put out this light or move that object!" What you have just done is simple: you have "opened a doorway" and allowed them to enter into the physical world—and future problems can and often do arise.

Simply put, it is not a good idea to try to "communicate" with ghosts through the Ouija board! According to Matthew Didier, Director of the Toronto Ghosts & Hauntings Research Society (TGHRS): "As a general rule, Ouija seems to exasperate the problems more than solve them. Regardless of my own beliefs and disbeliefs, the human mind is a powerful thing indeed. If someone wishes to believe strongly enough, almost anything will become true (if nothing else, at least to the person who believes.) It has been my overwhelming experience that an Ouija session almost inevitably leads to negative results. This could in part be caused by the way people pursue Ouija...Usually at night, in the dark and with an emphasis on atmosphere more than on actual contact and assuming a 'non-believer' says they are contacting nothing more than their subconscious, this situation would be ripe for the 'victims' to assume that they have now a dark and demonic presence with them then. Granted, one should remember that they are using a 'paranormal communication device' that is mass marketed by Parker Brothers."

www.ingramcontent.com/pod-product-compliance
Lightning Source LLC
Chambersburg PA
CBHW022247290526
45785CB00015B/384